W. Somerset Maugham

Twayne's English Authors Series

Kinley E. Roby, Editor

Northeastern University

TEAS 399

W. SOMERSET MAUGHAM
(1874–1965)
Photograph courtesy of Editta Sherman, New York

W. Somerset Maugham

By Forrest D. Burt

Texas A & M University

Twayne Publishers • *Boston*

for my wife, Veva;
my children, Cheree, Kevin, and Gingerlynn;
and my special friend, Milt

W. Somerset Maugham

Forrest D. Burt

Copyright © 1985 by G.K. Hall & Company
All Rights Reserved
Published by Twayne Publishers
A Division of G. K. Hall & Co.
A publishing subsidiary of ITT
70 Lincoln Street
Boston, Massachusetts 02111

Book Production by Elizabeth Todesco
Book Design by Barbara Anderson

Printed on permanent/durable acid-free
paper and bound in the United States of
America.

Library of Congress Cataloging in Publication Data

Burt, Forrest D.
   W. Somerset Maugham.

   (Twayne's English authors series; TEAS 399)
   Bibliography: p. 152
   Includes index.
   1. Maugham, W. Somerset (William Somerset), 1874–1965—
Criticism and interpretation. I. Title. II. Series.
PR6025.A86Z5585   1985   823'.912   84-25288
ISBN 0-8057-6885-8

Contents

About the Author
Preface
Chronology

> *Chapter One*
> Life and Background   1

> *Chapter Two*
> Pattern of Life   28

> *Chapter Three*
> Early Apprenticeship   40

> *Chapter Four*
> Later Apprenticeship   59

> *Chapter Five*
> Autobiographical Novel   71

> *Chapter Six*
> Works of Accomplishment   94

> *Chapter Seven*
> Artistic Excellence   115

> *Chapter Eight*
> Conclusion   134

Notes and References   143
Selected Bibliography   152
Index   155

About the Author

Forrest D. Burt is professor of English at Texas A&M University, where he has been a faculty member since 1967. He received his B.A. from Wayland Baptist University in 1962 and his M.A. in 1965 and the Ph.D. in 1967 from Texas Tech University. His articles and reviews, primarily in Victorian and Edwardian literature and psychology and literature, have appeared in the *Journal of Modern Literature*, *Journal of Individual Psychology*, the *Bulletin of Bibliography*, and *Literature and Psychology*. His books, mainly in rhetoric and evaluation of writing, have been published by Random House and the National Council of Teachers of English.

Preface

This work aims to serve as an introduction to the study of English literature and to the understanding of the writings of William Somerset Maugham. Although the focus is upon his literary works, the initial chapters deal with his life. Furthermore, throughout this study reference will be made to Maugham's life, his times, and other writers whenever such reference sheds light on the writings.

Critical study of this long-neglected writer has become more serious in the years following his death. In addition to the usual personal reminiscences, in the form of articles and books, that appear after the death of any popular writer, several scholarly and critically sound books have appeared. Raymond Toole Stott's last bibliography (1973), Charles Sanders's annotated bibliography of writings about Maugham, and Ted Morgan's biography are among these. In addition, several critical books—especially those by Calder, Curtis, Raphael, Dobrinsky, and Cordell—have strengthened this new serious consideration of Maugham.

The texts of the works are in exceptional order. The collected editions were nearly complete in Maugham's lifetime (see the bibliography below); and the recent reprint series of his original works published by Arno Press provides the basis for future studies.

I wish to acknowledge my debt to the many individuals who assisted me in this project. The library staffs at the Humanities Research Center at the University of Texas, Stanford University, Yale University, the Berg Collection at the New York Public Library, the Library of Congress, and Herbert J. Frost/W. Somerset Maugham Collection at Texas A & M University were all very helpful and deserve sincere thanks. Colleagues who have helped me include Stanley L. Archer, Jeanne Austin, Richard Hauer Costa, and Milton and Clara Huggett of Texas A & M University. Klaus Jonas of the University of Pittsburgh gave me honest advice. Richard A. Cordell of Purdue University, the leading American critic of Maugham since the thirties, helped and encouraged me in more ways than I could ever name. Joseph Dobrinsky of Montpellier University, the leading critic of Maugham in France today, took time to talk with me about our common interests in Maugham and shared his own work and ideas with me. Roger L. Brooks of Houston Baptist University deserves many thanks for encouraging me in my research in Victorian and Modern British literature and on Somerset Maugham. Special thanks must go also to Donald Dean Maddox (student, colleague, friend), to Milton Huggett, Stanley Archer, and Richard Hauer Costa (colleagues in Maugham study), to Kinley Roby (Twayne field editor), to Anne Jones, Emily McKeigue, and Athenaide Dallett (editors for G.K. Hall) for carefully reading my manuscript and helping me improve it, to Lewis DeSimone and Elizabeth Todesco (manuscript editor and production editor for G.K. Hall) for guiding this book through copyediting and production, and to Dean Keith Bryant and Dean W. David Maxwell of Texas A & M University, who assisted with released time and summer fellowships to work on this project. I thank Jeanna Boyer Sorrels for her part in typing the manuscript, and Nancy Snyder Boller especially for her typing and encouragement. I am grateful to my children—Cheree, Kevin, and Gingerlynn—for their understanding and concern. And above all I am grateful to my wife, Veva, for her constant love and support.

Forrest D. Burt

Texas A & M University

Chronology

1874   William Somerset Maugham born at the British Embassy in Paris on 25 January, the fourth son of English parents.

1882   Mother dies of tuberculosis.

1884   Father dies of cancer.

1887   Enters King's School, Canterbury.

1891   Spends one year and several months in Germany.

1892–1897   Attends medical school at St. Thomas's Hospital in London; receives an M.D. degree.

1897   *Liza of Lambeth,* a naturalistic novel based largely on his medical experience in Lambeth.

1898   *The Making of a Saint,* a historical novel.

1899   *Orientations: Short Stories.*

1902   *Mrs. Craddock: A Novel.*

1905   *The Land of the Blessed Virgin: Sketches and Impressions in Andalusia,* a travel book.

1906   Begins love affair with Sue Jones.

1907   *Lady Frederick,* his first successful play, begins a performance run of over a year at the Royal Court Theatre in London.

1913   Sue Jones rejects Maugham's proposal of marriage.

1914–1915   Serves with a British ambulance unit and with military intelligence in Geneva.

1915   *Of Human Bondage,* autobiographical fiction.

1916   Visits South Sea islands; gathers material on Paul Gauguin for *The Moon and Sixpence.*

1917   Serves as the chief agent in Russia for the British and American secret services in an attempt to prevent the Bolshevik coup of 1917. Contracts tuberculosis and spends time in a sanitorium. Marries Syrie Wellcome.

1919   *The Moon and Sixpence,* based on the life of Paul Gauguin.

1921   *The Circle,* a comedy of manners, begins a run of 181 performances at the Haymarket Theatre in London.

1928   *Ashenden,* short stories based upon Maugham's secret service experiences.

1929   Syrie Wellcome divorces Maugham.

1930   *Cakes and Ale,* a novel in the comic tradition.

1938   *The Summing Up,* an autobiographical sketch of his life and work. Visits India.

1940–1946   Spends war years in the United States.

1944   *The Razor's Edge,* a novel drawing from his visit to India.

1946   Donates the *Of Human Bondage* manuscript and the earlier unpublished version of this work, *"The Artistic Temperament of Stephen Carey,"* to the Library of Congress.

1962   *Purely For My Pleasure,* description of his art collection with an account of how each piece was acquired. "Looking Back" (in *Show*), an autobiographical sketch of parts of his life.

1965   Maugham dies at his Villa Mauresque on 16 December at the age of ninety-one.

Chapter One
Life and Background

Childhood in Paris

On 25 January 1874 William Somerset Maugham was born in the British Embassy in Paris—thereby ensuring his citizenship in the British Empire, then under the reign of Queen Victoria. His father, Robert Ormond Maugham, an English lawyer in the Paris firm of Maugham and Sewall, was serving at the time as a legal attaché to the British Embassy. He was fifty years old and William was his eighth child. Maugham's mother, Edith Mary Snell Maugham, the daughter of an English army officer and of a mother who wrote French novels and light music, was much admired by prominent Parisians for her beauty and charm. She was only twenty-nine years old. William was the fourth of her living children, all sons.

Maugham's father traveled extensively and owned a large library of travel books. His own father had been an eminent barrister and author, had established the Incorporated Law Society, and had founded and edited the *Legal Observer,* later the *Solicitor's Journal* (accomplishments that entitled him to be called the "Father of Legal Journalism").[1] For some reason, unknown even to his own son, Maugham's father moved to Paris. Perhaps, Maugham once speculated, his father was drawn by the same "restlessness for the unknown as had consumed his son" (*SU,* 15). A "connoisseur in art as well as law,"[2] he was considered not attractive—"ugly," according to Maugham. He did enjoy an active social life—for which his attractive young wife was an asset. As Maugham reports, "they were known in the Paris of the day as Beauty and the Beast" (*SU,* 16).

Famous for her beauty and charm, Edith Mary Snell Maugham was known also for her salon where writers, artists, and politicians could meet.[3] According to Maugham's brother Frederic—eight years his senior—"it is hardly an exaggeration to say that she knew almost everyone worth knowing in Paris."[4] Her interest in art and literature was genuine; she was a "great novel reader" with cases full of books (*SU,* 17). And, according to Frederic, on rainy days they "generally went to the Louvre or to the Luxembourg." A child of English parents, she had been born in India where her father served as a major in the army. Her father was killed in battle shortly after she was born. Like her sons, she spoke two languages as a child—"Hindustani much better than English." She was sent at a very early age to school in England. When she and Robert met, she and her mother were living in Paris on her father's pension. Maugham's brother remembers her in this way: "In my mind's eye the gracious figure of my mother, who was a very beautiful woman, is still to be seen moving about and speaking pleasant words to her boys and watching over our happiness."[5] Maugham, as Frederic Raphael states, "never ceased to adore her."[6]

The Maughams, therefore, led an active and busy life in Paris. Maugham's father left early in the morning and did not return until around seven, and generally worked on Saturdays as well. But there was time for laughter in the Maugham's lives. Frederic recalls: "In my youth I often heard, both from my parents and others, of the gaiety, the *joie de vivre* and the genial spirit of the French in the days of the Empire, which made Paris the most attractive place of residence in all Europe. A large number of English people had apartments in Paris and were welcomed as friends of the French people. There was a lot of entertaining and much innocent enjoyment. . . ."[7] And the Maughams were evidently happily married. One of Mrs. Maugham's friends, Lady Anglesey, an American, once told William that she had one day asked her: "You're so beautiful and there are so many people in love with you, why are you faithful to that ugly little man you've married?" She replied, "He never hurts my feelings" (*SU*, 16). And Frederic remembers the wonderful days of their vacations when, although his father could not go with them because of his work, he would join them later. On one occasion, he recalls, his father arrived "with a machine, afterwards to be known as a boneshaker, on which we all learnt a surprisingly rapid means of motion. . . . It had iron tyres and practically no spring under the saddle, but the riders of that day . . . did not complain." And if "it was warm in Paris and we were still there we used to bathe very frequently in the Seine in one of the wooden floating bath structures made for the purpose."[8]

The world that Maugham was born into, however, had begun a major alteration from that which Frederic had known. Four years before Maugham's birth, France was at war, Paris was under siege, and the Maughams were forced to leave for England until it was safe to return. Maugham's father's "life was greatly affected by the war of 1870; for his practice was ruined and had to be built up again in a Paris to which many of his old clients never returned."⁹ Having to work long hours—leaving early and returning late—he made no great impact on Maugham's life. No wonder Maugham would write: "My father was a stranger to me."¹⁰ When Maugham was born in 1874, both his parents were in bad health. His mother suffered from tuberculosis. She was often ill, and always failing. Maugham "shared a room with his French nurse, but often was able to spend a little time alone with his mother in her bedroom in the mornings and was welcome in the salon. . . ." Soon his older brothers were off to school at Dover in England. They returned on the three holiday periods, of course. But otherwise, the young Maugham had the Paris world all to himself. It is not surprising, then, that he had "the illusion of being an only child." Frederic Raphael describes Maugham's life at that time as "a life of cosseted indulgence with two parents who cared much for each other."¹¹ Still at age sixty-four Maugham wrote that he knew "Little of them [his parents] but from hearsay" (*SU,* 15). As business worsened and bad health took its toll and life altered, it was no doubt his French nurse who became more and more his constant companion and who gave the small boy constant love.

Death of Parents and Move to England

Life altered quite suddenly. The only remedy for his mother's condition, the doctors maintained, was another pregnancy. In 1892, the child was born dead and Mrs. Maugham died six days later. Maugham then had only his nurse, and his father—who was a stranger to him.

Two years later life altered once more—in three telling events. First, his father, whose health declined steadily as he struggled to maintain his business, kept up the building of a vacation house he had begun earlier, and grieved over the loss of his wife, died of cancer and overwork. The money he left was barely enough to educate his four sons. Maugham was ten years old.

Of course, Maugham's brothers felt the loss deeply also. Frederic called it tragic—the deaths of their mother in 1882 and their father in 1884—"tragic for young boys and greatly altering their lives." "It was the end of a home. My brothers and I were soon separated by force of events, and therefore we did not see much of each other."¹²

But Maugham was the youngest. His life would be more severely altered.

The second event, a consequence of the first, was that Maugham—now an orphan—accompanied by his French nurse, was soon shipped to England, his native land, whose language he could hardly speak. This change would cut a deep groove in Maugham's memory. As Raphael observes, "The French influence on his character and style can scarcely be overemphasized. French locutions always haunted his prose and French literature was to be closer to his heart than . . . English. . . ."[13] The boys' guardians were a London solicitor, Albert Dixon—"a kindly man who did his best" for them—and their uncle, their father's only surviving brother, Henry Macdonald Maugham, vicar of Whitstable, married but with no children. It was to the vicar's home that Maugham went. There could not have been a household any more unsuitable for the ten-year-old French-speaking Maugham. Frederic states: "I am afraid he [their uncle] was very narrow-minded and a far from intelligent cleric, and I cannot truthfully praise him as a guardian of boys."[14] In the home of his uncle and aunt, Maugham "found himself a stranger in a strange land, at the chilly mercy of a cowed *Hausfrau* and her snobbish, joyless husband, a childless couple no happier to see him than he was to see them."[15]

Perhaps the most tragic event of all, though, was his uncle's announcement that his nurse, the only other survivor from the lost Parisian paradise of his childhood, was to be sent away the next day. He had shared a room with her. She had been the one constant companion through the last several years of his childhood. She was all that was left of his home. In his old age, in "Looking Back"—published when he was eighty-eight years old—Maugham spoke of this loss. He wrote in his usual unsentimental manner, and in such a modest and simple fashion that a reader could easily miss the force of his grief. He first states: "My father died years later [after his mother] and I was taken by my nurse to England to be delivered over to my uncle and guardian who was Vicar of Whitstable." There can be little doubt that Maugham's use of passive construction here is deliberate. Then, following this statement, is the poignant sentence: "I loved my nurse and shed bitter tears when she was there and then sent away" (*L,* 64). It was a loss from which he would never recover. And even here in these early years, Maugham learned the power of money—which he would call the sixth sense without which one can not enjoy the other five: his uncle stopped payment and the nurse he loved was gone. He would never again surrender himself as completely, take such risks, be hurt so deeply.

In the early, unpublished, autobiographical novel, "The Artistic Temperament of Stephen Carey," his uncle tells him that his mother was always throwing money away, that after debts were paid little money was left, and that it is almost a blessing that she died. But even the nurse herself in this early version of *Of Human Bondage* is mainly concerned with the position she is losing, whether she will get a whole month's notice, and who will get Mrs. Carey's clothes. In *The Summing Up,* Maugham writes of his losses: "When I was a small boy and unhappy I used to dream night after night that my life at school was a dream and that I should wake to find myself at home again with my mother." The alterations to his life were permanent:

I have long ceased to have that dream; but I have never quite lost the sense that my living life was a mirage in which I did this and that because that was how it fell out, but which, even while I was playing my part in it, I could look at from a distance and know it for the mirage it was. When I look back on my life, with its successes and its failures, its endless errors, its deceptions and its fulfilments, its joys and miseries, it seems to me strangely lacking in reality. It is shadowy and unsubstantial. (*SU,* 304)

And yet Maugham found that he did have some control over his life and the reactions of others, that there was some freedom in bondage. Philip, in the autobiographical *Of Human Bondage* (1915) (and Stephen, in the earlier version of that novel) discovers pleasure in pain, a kind of pleasurable sensation in seeing others feel pity for the sufferer. Ted Morgan suggests that Maugham's experiences at the vicarage established a crucial link between love and suffering: "The death of his mother had forged it, and it would appear not only in his work but in all of his important relationships."[16]

Development of a Stammer

Another consequence of Maugham's loss of home and the move to England was his developing a speech impediment, a stammer, which he did not have in France and which he would have, although later improved, throughout his long life. It began when he came to England at the age of ten.[17] It may well have been, as Morgan suggests, "an expression of juvenile insecurity of his first stumbling efforts in a new environment . . . the expression of a conflict between giving himself and holding back."[18] Or it may have been, as Anthony Curtis suggests, "the outward and audible sign" of his alienation.[19] But if stammering is "a manifestation of a fear to speak the truth to oneself or about oneself to another,"[20] then it may be that in his hesitancy and frustration, Maugham knew, as did the novelist Edward Driffield in *Cakes and Ale,* that truth was not always well received. He would have to become a writer to tell the truth with the simplicity and spontaneity that he so strongly believed should characterize all communication—but which he was never able to master in his own oral communication. In his writing he found that peace and fluency to such an extent that when he was almost ninety years old he could say: "I have never been so happy or so much at ease as when, seated at my table, from my pen flowed word after word until the luncheon gong forced me to put an end to the day's work" (*L,* 62). Maugham was himself aware of the specific relationship between difficulty in speaking and a need to write. In his preface to Arnold Bennett's novel *The Old Wives' Tale,* he said of Bennett, a fellow stammerer: "It may be that except for the stammer which forced him to introspection, Arnold would never have become a writer."[21]

Interesting at this point are the findings of speech research that stammers tend to be found "most frequently in those families that place a high premium upon the truth and then punish its verbalization."[22] This description could quite well fit the home Maugham's uncle dominated. And it was in his new home in England that Maugham began to stammer.[23]

Educated at London University and Oriel College, Oxford, the Reverend Macdonald Maugham, Maugham's only living uncle on his father's side of the family, had been vicar of Whitstable for thirteen years when William arrived in 1884. In 1858, some twenty-six years before this arrival date, he had married Barbara Sophia von Scheidlen, the daughter of a German banker. They had no children. As would be expected, the Maughams were prominent citizens in this class-conscious sea resort and fishing village. They employed two maids—as well as other servants, traded at the "right" shops, and lived just the life proper for a vicar and his wife.

Maugham has written five accounts of his experiences in Whitstable: Stephen Carey's in "The Artistic Temperament of Stephen Carey" (ca. 1898), Philip Carey's in *Of Human Bondage* (1915), Willie Ashenden's in *Cakes and Ale* (1930), and Maugham's own in *The Summing Up* (1938) and "Looking Back" (1962). Although similar to the first two, the account in the last work is not fictionalized and captures the atmosphere of the vicar's home with the directness and poignancy necessary for one to understand the conditions in which his stammer developed:

On my first Sunday in England I accompanied my uncle and his wife, my aunt, to church for the morning service. . . . When the service was at last at an end we drove back to the vicarage and had dinner. After the table was cleared and I was deposited on a chair at one end of it and my uncle, with a prayer book open at the proper place, put it in front of me and told me to learn the collect of the day by heart. "I'll hear you say it at at teatime," he said, "and if you say it properly you shall have a piece of cake." Then he went into his study to rest after the morning's exertions and my aunt went to lie down in the drawing room. I was left alone. An hour or so later my aunt went into the garden to have a stroll and as she passed the dining room windows, peeped in to see how I was getting on. My face was buried in my hands and I was crying, crying bitterly. She hurried into the dining room and asked me what was the matter. Crying all the more, I sobbed, "I can't understand it. All those words, I don't know what they mean." "Oh, Willie," she said, "your uncle wouldn't want you to cry. It was for your own good that he wanted you to learn the collect. Don't cry." She took the prayer book away from me and I was left alone once more to sob my heart out. When the table was set for tea my uncle did not speak to me. I could see that he was very cross. (*L,* 64)

With this strange new home and with his stammer, it is understandable that Maugham would believe so strongly in the importance of clarity in communication.

In this setting, then, Maugham began to sense his separateness from others and began to be more an observer than a participant. Even on shopping days, "as he tagged along in the wake of his aunt, Willie registered indelible impressions of these people. One of the most memorable was Gilbert Saunders, the bank manager of Hammond and Co.'s bank, and his uncle's church warden. . . . Sophie was in the habit of concluding her shopping by a gossip with his sister. . . ." They would typically "resume shopping and then perhaps go down one of the sidestreets, where fishermen were mending their nets, to gaze for a moment or two at the sea before returning to the Vicarage."[24] Perhaps the deepest impression upon him, though, was made by the class structure evident at every turn, those who were the "right" people, and those who were not. Even Mary Ann, his aunt and uncle's maid in *Cakes and Ale* (and in *Of Human Bondage*), adheres rigidly to this system. Speaking of Willie's reprimand for riding his bicycle with the Driffields, not the "right" people, she says, "I don't blame your uncle . . . I wouldn't let you go about with them, not if you was my nephew. Fancy their asking you to ride your bicycle with them. Some people will do anything."[25]

No doubt Maugham's interpretation of this life would have been different if his background had not been what it was. Life then could possibly have been as Morgan suggests: "it cannot have been such a bad life. He was living in a seaside resort, the ward of a local dignitary. The air was clean and the food was good. He did not have to compete with other children for the affection of his aunt and uncle."[26] But a sense of home, of love, a fluency in speaking—these he did not have. Therefore he was, as Morgan adds, "quite miserable."

Understandably, he became an avid reader and lived actively in an imaginary world. He would "feast his eyes upon pictures of mosques and minarets, palaces and terraces, pillars and grottoes as he pursued the memoirs of travellers in the East. His greatest find was the . . . *Thousand and One Arabian Nights* which he devoured; then there was Scott's Waverley Novels to be got through, Lewis Carroll. . . ."[27] So, when it was arranged that he, still but ten years old, should go to preparatory school, he had read "most of the Waverley novels, W. W. Lane's 'Arabian Nights,' 'Alice in Wonderland,' and 'Through the looking glass' " (L, 64).

The Experience of School

That was his preparation for English schools. He had read, had observed his fellow human beings, had curiosity and imagination, had a command of two languages. But he had never held a bat or kicked a football. Little did he know what to expect that first day when he arrived with his uncle, fearful and knowing he would stammer, to meet the headmaster of King's School, Canterbury. As they waited in the parlor for the headmaster to come out and take charge of him, he said, "Tell him I stammer, Uncle." Looking back on that moment in his old age he wrote: "I little knew then how great an influence on my life this impediment of mine would have" (L, 64).

But the headmaster, the Reverend George Blore, "did nothing to reassure his tongue-tied new pupil."[28] For, in addition to encountering the "practical cruelty of the English schoolboy,"[29] Maugham would have to "suffer the verbal whips and scorns of the teaching staff." "There is no evidence that Maugham was ever caned, although his name is on record as appearing in the school's Black Book in which pupils' misdemeanours were recorded." He would never forget "the moment when he suffered a total verbal paralysis while construing Latin in front of the irascible Reverend B. B. Gordon. . . ."[30] Indeed, far from forgetting that moment, Maugham when nearly ninety years old would recall it with such vividness that he could write:

The Latin was simple and I knew very well how to put it in English, but I was shy and nervous. I began to stammer. One of the boys started to giggle, then another, then a third, and in a minute or two the whole class was shouting, screaming, yelling with laughter. I pretended not to notice, but went on stammering my head off. At last the master thumped the table at which he sat with his clenched fist and, shouting to be heard in the uproar, yelled, "Sit down, you fool, I don't know why they put you in this form." I sat down. I was dazed—but not for long. I was enraged: I could have killed the man. I was helpless, I could do nothing. . . . (*L,* 64)

It was from this experience that Maugham's life altered once more:

I made up my mind, then and there, that I would never spend another term with that beast of a master. I knew exactly what to do. I was small for my age and frail, but cunning. I had no difficulty in persuading my uncle that with my delicate health it would be safer for me to spend the following winter again with the tutor at Hyeres rather than take the risk of another winter in the cold and damp Canterbury, with the happy result that at the end of that mortifying term I left the King's School for good. (*L,* 64)

What is of great importance in these experiences is how Maugham perceived and remembered them—which may or may not be how they actually were or were seen by others. In fact, as Curtis observes, "if one turns to the testimony of others who were at The King's School near to the time of Maugham it does not seem to be quite such a terrible place; purgatorial shall we say, rather than positively hellish."[31] And it is interesting that Maugham's brothers a few years earlier had also encountered difficulties at school at Dover for which their French background had not prepared them. Frederic wrote:

My brothers and I were at first called "froggies" since we came from Paris and, I suspect, wore French clothes. Nor does a boy know of his own peculiarities of speech. It took me many years to acquire an English pronunciation of a good many words derived from the French; I still cannot without deliberation pronounce (or mispronounce) the words "liqueur" or "blouse" or "landau" and other French words as an Englishman does. Schoolboys have a natural dislike for the unusual in other boys.[32]

But his brothers were able to overcome their difficulties quite easily. They were older when their parents died, when their home came to an end. And they did not stammer. Also, they could play games.

At King's School, however, Maugham refined and developed his powers of observation and his distinctive way of relating to others. As Curtis observes, "He soon discovered where his real power lay—in the accuracy of his insights. If he suffered wounds he was capable of inflicting them. His tongue was as sharp, if not sharper, than anyone's. On the whole he remained an outsider, . . . a confirmed bookworm, but when he was old enough to share a study he formed the first of those relations, the beginning of that impulse to form possessive and exclusive attachments, that brought so much misery in later life."[33] That posture of being a detached, critical—even cynical—observer would serve him well in his career as a writer. In his 1948 analysis of modern literature, Cyril Connolly would place Maugham with Maupassant in the role of "The Incorruptible Observer," one of the four roles assumed by modern artists who sense their alienation from nonartists.[34] Maugham would always be keenly conscious of how different he was from others. He would remain more of an observer than a participant. He would always feel separate from others.

Maugham's decision to leave King's School was one that would alter his life dramatically. He would not have the education and personal associations with fellow university-trained writers. Although he has often written about the consequences of this decision, he never did so with greater clarity than in "Looking Back":

I have sometimes amused myself by wondering what my life would have been if that master had not been the brute he was and I had remained at school. The end of term exams had brought me from the bottom of the form to within six or seven of the top and after another term I should have been moved into the sixth. Then with a scholarship I should in due course have gone up to Cambridge as my brothers had done. It is just possible that I might have been elected to a fellowship . . . though with my stammer I could not have been much use as a tutor or a lecturer. (L, 66)

His decision made, he was soon off to Germany and to experiences that would alter his life in new ways.

The German Experience

With the assistance of his Aunt Sophie, Maugham was soon situated in Heidelberg. He "warmed from the first to the place with its ancient university, its tree-lined streets and its ruined *schloss.* . . . He also found much to stimulate him in his encounters with the infinite variety of student and professional life with which Heidelberg teemed at the end of the nineteenth century."[35] The sixteen-year-old Maugham had a room in Frau von Gaubau's pension. He learned German, attended Kuno Fisher's lectures at the University of Heidelberg, saw performances of Ibsen, and listened to Wagner. His reading broadened and expanded: Fielding, Meredith, Swinburne, Verlaine, Pater, Arnold, Dante, Fitzgerald's *Omar Khayyam,* Newman.

It was in Heidelberg that Maugham became an "eager apprentice of civilized learning."[36] And it was there, according to Morgan, that he "first knew the delights of conversations, with interminable talks about art and literature, and free will and determinism, and discovered commonplaces that each teenage boy discovers as if for the first time."[37]

Two of his new friends at this time, a Harvard Greek professor and an aesthete who had studied law and attended Cambridge, would have a profound influence on his life. With the former, Maugham went on long walks in "the fir-clad hills, to the top of the Konigstuhl, where he saw stretching below him the plain of the Neckar, and took notice for the first time of the beauty that surrounds him."[38]

When the Harvard professor left Heidelberg, his place was taken by Brooks, who "on coming down from Cambridge, had spent a dissolute year in London and was come to Germany in search of culture." In "Looking Back," his last work, Maugham gives the following account of their early friendship: "We went for long walks together and he talked to me of Cardinal Newman, George Meredith, the Pater of the 'Imaginary Portraits,' Swinburne and Omar Khayyam. He had written out the quatrains in longhand, I suppose because the book was expensive and this was before the days of the typewriter, and used to read passages to me. I was thrilled" (*L,* 65).

It was not until later, Maugham states, "that it dawned upon me that the trouble these two men took to keep me interested was due not to the fact that I listened to their conversation entranced nor to any kindness they may have felt for a lonely, ignorant boy of sixteen, but to their concupiscence" (*L,* 66). Brooks not only guided his reading and thinking and left him with a genuine love of literature, but he also led him to have his first homosexual experience, according to Ted Morgan. Even while at King's School Maugham's "homosexual inclinations had begun to show themselves . . . when his avoidance of participation in competitive games isolated him from his peer group—forming strong passions for boys who had the qualities he lacked." With Brooks, according to Morgan's source, Glenway Wescott, Maugham had his "first full sexual experience . . . with a man ten years his senior." Maugham was drawn to him "not only physically but also by his shunning of convention, his pose as a man of letters, and his intention of devoting himself to beauty." This experience formed Maugham's basic sexual preference throughout his life. Although he would have an affair with Sue Jones (daughter of the dramatist Henry Arthur Jones and model for Rosie in *Cakes and Ale*) that lasted eight years, would marry and have a daughter, Maugham would prefer and return to his homosexual relations—with Gerald Haxton, Alan Searle, and others. And when Maugham left Heidelberg, in 1892, he returned to an England in which there was every reason to be secretive about his sexual preference: a new law making the practice of homosexuality a criminal offense.[39]

Orphaned, friendless, deprived of parental love, the young Maugham was a prime candidate for the type of repression that leads to stammering and difficulties in sexual identity. Not the strongest drive—hunger, pain, fear are generally considered stronger—sex nevertheless is so attacked and inhibited that in modern society "conscience and custom weigh most heavily" upon it. "The culture demands for all practical purposes a completely sexless child."[40] It is typical, then, for anxiety and repression to occur in such situations as Maugham's at the vicarage and at King's School.

Difficulties in identifying one's sexual role frequently occur in such situations. The psychologist Alfred Adler maintained that "everyone has, inherent in his being, both maleness and femaleness. The healthy individual is able to separate the two and adopt the one appropriate for his biological sex." The unhealthy individual lives a kind of "double life," partaking of both masculine and feminine aspects of his or her being.[41] And to add to Maugham's anxiety and need to conceal was the event, in his third year in London, 1895, of Oscar Wilde's arrest for homosexuality. Impressing its consequences upon many homosexuals of that time, the event served as an unforgettable reminder to Maugham of the need to conceal much of his private life, especially his homosexual tendencies.[42]

Loss of Faith

Maugham, the agnostic and skeptic who arrived in London from Heidelberg in 1892, never softened into a trusting, believing individual—despite a lifelong search and longing to do so. Belief in God was now beyond him. Biblical scholars maintain that the Aramaic word *Abba* for "Father" in the Lord's Prayer ("Our Father who art in Heaven") is a word whose meaning and whose very sound connotes intimacy and tenderness.[43] Maugham had no basis in his experience for such trust. To pray such a prayer, to trust, to believe, would prove difficult for him. His father was so absent from his life and unrelated to his world that Maugham had no such model. Understandably, he threw off his faith in God and became skeptical of the goodness of others, of friendships and love. Maugham would conclude:

There is no reason for life and life has no meaning. We are here, inhabitants for a little while of a small planet, revolving round a moon or star which in turn is a member of one of unnumbered galaxies. (*SU, 272*).

The only God that is of use is a being who is personal, supreme and good, and whose existence is as certain as that two and two make four. I cannot penetrate the mystery. I remain an agnostic and the practical outcome of agnosticism is that you act as though God did not exist. (*SU, 260*)

Essentially, then, when Maugham arrived in London in 1892 he had made the choices that he would carry throughout life. And Maugham's was a life that held considerable mystery. When Christopher Isherwood met Maugham in 1941, he worded his puzzlement in a letter to E. M. Forster: "he reminds me of an old Gladstone bag covered with labels, God only knows what is inside."[44] A year after Maugham's death, Noel Coward wrote: "he was a complex man and his view of his fellow creatures was jaundiced, to say the least. . . . With all his brilliance and verbal clarity, he rarely drew a sympathetic character—probably, I suspect, because he quite genuinely believed that no such phenomenon existed . . . he has little faith in the human heart. . . ."[45] Maugham wrote of life as he observed and experienced it.

Believing, as did Oscar Wilde, that "a life might be fabricated like a work of art,"[46] he set out to design a pattern for his life. Maugham's critics describe his design in different ways: a pattern of deception, a quest for freedom, a yearning for God—all, of course, shedding some light upon the nature of his style of life. But the most significant pattern that emerges, it seems, is a pattern of compensation, a pattern of compensating for his life in his writing. What he experienced as being negative, a weakness, a limitation in life he turned to a positive characteristic, a strength, as he compensated for his limitations in his writing. For instance, in life he never completely overcame his stammer, never developed fluency in speaking. But in his writing he never stopped revising a work until it met his standards of simplicity, clarity, euphony, until it was spontaneous and natural. In his sexual life he betrayed an ambivalence—with a preference for a homosexual relationship—and by his own admission never experienced mutual love (*SU*, 77). However, in his writing he demonstrated a profound understanding of the relationship between men and women, and of the importance of the masculine and feminine roles in marriage.

And in his own life, he never returned to his childhood faith in God: "Some say that God has placed evils here for our training; . . . that he has sent them upon men to punish them for their sins. But I have seen a child die of meningitis" (*SU*, 264), he wrote. But there was within Maugham, according to many critics, a yearning to believe in such a God—especially as he grew older. As Karl Pfeiffer observed in 1959, Maugham had obstacles in the way of his belief: "his skeptical, rational turn of mind; his keen sense of irony; his feeling that conversion would be only a cowardly fear."[47] Maugham speculated about himself: "It may be that in my heart, having found rest nowhere, I had some deep ancestral craving for God and immortality which my reason would have no truck with" (*SU*, 309). It is in his writing, though, that Maugham searched most intensely for meaning, for a sense of purpose. In life, Maugham was orphaned young, was lonely, was deprived of parental love. He wrote: "It is one of the faults of my nature that I have suffered more from the pains, than I have enjoyed the pleasures of my life" (*SU*, 282). But in his writing, he shows pity and tolerance for the weaknesses and tragedies of human beings—a quality that Richard Heron Ward, an early English critic and biographer, termed his most "characteristic quality."[48]

Therefore, Maugham could honestly say: "I have put the whole of my life into my books" (*SU*, 10):

I have been attached, deeply attached, to a few people; but I have been interested in men in general not for their own sakes, but for the sake of my work. I have, not as Kant enjoined, regarded each man as an end in himself, but as material that might be useful to me as a writer. (*SU,* 7–8)

My natural inclination has been to keep aloof from every kind of public activity. . . . Thinking that not the whole of life was long enough to learn to write well, I have been unwilling to give to other activities time that I so much need to achieve the purpose I had in mind. I have never been able intimately to persuade myself that anything else mattered. (*SU,* 229)

Psychologist Rollo May speaks of this type of compensation as a way of distinguishing an individual who is an artist from one who is neurotic: "Both artist and neurotic speak and live from subconscious and unconscious depths of their society. The artist however does this positively, communicating what he experiences to his fellow men . . . living out, in forms that only he can create, the depths of unconsciousness which he experiences in his own being as he struggles and molds his world."[49] Of course, Maugham was aware of much of this pattern. He wrote: "We writers generally do not write because we want to; we write because we must. There may be other things in the world that more pressingly want doing: we must liberate our souls of the burden of creation" (*SU,* 230).

Career Decision

When Maugham returned to Whitstable in 1892 from a year in Heidelberg, there was the question of what he would do with his life. His London guardian, Dixon, arranged for him to have a trial period in an accounting firm. But it did not work out. The problem unsolved, Maugham returned to Whitstable and to the home his uncle dominated. At this point his uncle had little patience with him: "He thought me incompetent. Which I was, and lazy, which I wasn't," Maugham wrote. The local doctor then came to the rescue: suggesting that he go into medicine. The idea appealed to Maugham, "chiefly because it would enable me to live in London, which I very much wanted to do. . . ." So, at the age of eighteen I entered St. Thomas Hospital as a medical student" (*L,* 66).

There he was with students of about his own age—except for those who had gone to Oxford or Cambridge for a couple of years—"who looked upon themselves as a cut above the rest of us who hadn't been to a university" (*L,* 66). Maugham was considered a "shy, retiring, aloof, and almost forbidding individual who was always seen with but one friend."[50] At St. Thomas's Maugham spent five years of his youth, from 1892 (age eighteen) to 1897 (age twenty-three), when he received his M.D. degree. From the first he never intended to practice medicine, unless, of course, he had to. He wanted to be a writer.

He wrote constantly, keeping a notebook, "in the style of Oscar Wilde," with quotes from his landlady, notes on his observations, and ideas that occurred to him.[51] In his early youth, Maugham wrote Ibsenite plays that "delved into the secrets of the human soul." He felt that his best chance for the theater was to write two or three novels that would give him the reputation to induce the managers to look favorably at his plays. Believing writing as serious as life, he approached it with a determined purpose. By early 1896 (age twenty-two), he had completed two short stories, "A Bad Example" and "Daisy."[52] These were not accepted for publication. He was, however, encouraged by one publisher to write a longer work of fiction. It was called *Liza of Lambeth,* a story based on his experiences as a young doctor in the Lambeth slums. This, his first novel, was published in 1897, the same year he received his degree. It had a modest success. Needless to say, he gave up medicine. He wrote: "At the end of five years I was qualified and, having just brought out a novel called 'Liza of Lambeth,' which had a *success de scandale,* I decided to abandon medicine and earn my living as an author" (*L,* 67).

Perhaps more important than that success and his decision to abandon a career in medicine was the fact that with this novel Maugham moved closer to his goal of having plays produced. Not only had he launched a career as a novelist, which he had planned, he also was able to demonstrate many of his dramatic skills. When Henry Arthur Jones, "the most popular playwright of the 1890's,"[53] read this novel, he told a friend that in "due course" (which turned out to be ten years) Maugham should become "one of the most successful dramatists of the day." Perhaps in it he saw, Maugham speculates, a "directness and an effective way of presenting a scene that suggested a sense of the theatre" (*SU,* 18). That interest in writing for the theater began in Heidelberg when he first was taken by the plays of Ibsen, a writer he imitated in his early attempts at playwriting. In this light, it is interesting that "The Artistic Temperament of Stephen Carey"[54] opens with Stephen (Philip in the later novel) alone, playing with his toy theater, creating a play of his own. And later at school, in a letter to his uncle, he asks how his *theater* is doing. Maugham's interest and talent in drama were to become important in his career.

London

With the reception of his first novel came invitations to luncheons, dinners, and parties. Literary ladies began to ask him to their homes. There he met writers, politicians, and artists in an atmosphere not unlike that which his mother had created years before in Paris. Late in his life Maugham wrote:

I have often wondered since why those rich and worldly people bothered about me. I had precious little to offer. I was poor and shy; I stammered; and I knew nothing about the sorts of things they talked about. . . . Many, many years later I asked one of the hostesses of my youth what she and others had seen in me that they were so kind to me. "You were different from other young men," she said. "Though quiet and silent, you had a sort of restless vitality that was intriguing." (*L,* 67)

One home to which he often was invited was that of arch-Victorian Augustus Hare, undeniably a first-class "snob"—but such a unique and fascinating "snob"[55]—serving as a model for this character type in many of Maugham's works: Alroy Kear, for instance, in *Cakes and Ale,* and Elliott Templeton in *The Razor's Edge.* And it was in such settings that Maugham began his advanced study and observation of individuals—always, of course, for the sake of his work. Believing that one should write in the fashion of one's period, not that of the past, and that "language is alive and constantly changing," he knew that he must avoid artificiality at all costs. Forty years later he would state: "I would sooner a writer were vulgar than mincing; for life is vulgar, and it is life he seeks" (*SU,* 31). It would take Maugham some years, though, before he was able to develop the confidence to write simply and concisely and with the knowledge that comes only from experience, the knowledge that a writer must have to write about a subject with understanding. Later he would put this truth in this way: "To produce a great picture, it is necessary not merely for the artist to prepare his canvas, but prepare himself."[56] And "the production of a work of art is not the result of a miracle. It requires preparation. . . . All the power of the artist's mind must be set to work on it, all his technical skill, all his experience, and whatever he has in him of character and individuality, so that with infinite pains he may present it with the completeness that is fitting to it" (*SU,* 95). Maugham believed much as Oscar Wilde did that the "artist's duty was to give free play to sensation and temptation so as to experience more of them and escape submission to any single one."[57] Maugham wrote: "I desired to feel the common human lot. I saw no reason to subordinate the claims of sense to the tempting lure of spirit, and I was determined to get whatever fulfillment I could out of social intercourse and human relations, out of food, drink and fornication, luxury, sport, art, travel. . . . But it was an effort . . ." (*SU*, 88–89). Accordingly, he traveled, made friends, took risks—all for the sake of his work. He was eager to experience life.

Apprenticeship

In the first part of his apprenticeship, from 1897 (the publication of his first novel) to 1907 (the date of his first successful play), Maugham made several experiments, as well as several mistakes, but he never failed to learn quickly. His second novel was called *The Making of a Saint*—a very unsimple, unclear, demanding story of the Italian Renaissance, published in 1898. This work concerned a subject that he did not know well. Realizing his mistake, Maugham would not allow it to be reissued during his lifetime. Another example is *The Land of The Blessed Virgin,* which he wrote the same year. In this work he made a different mistake: writing in a style that was not simple, but overly decorative; seeking richness of language before clarity of meaning, yielding to the intoxicating sound of beautiful words. After Maugham rewrote the novel again and again, it was finally published in 1905.[58] But even revised, it shows Maugham in the grip of a very elevated style. The same year, 1898, he published his first short story, "The Punctiliousness of Don Sebastian," in *Cosmopolis*. The following year he published *Orientations,* a collection of short stories that included the two rejected, the one just published, and two others. Also, in 1899 Maugham rewrote "The Artistic Temperament of Stephen Carey"—which he had written the year before. Fortunately he found no publisher for it. These works were followed by two novels: *The Hero* (1900), based on the Boer War, and *Mrs. Craddock* (1902), a novel of an unhappy marriage. Summing up his work to this point, Maugham wrote: "I worked steadily, I published two or three novels and a volume of short stories; I wrote a number of plays which no manager would accept. One of my novels, *Mrs. Craddock* had a modest success . . . " (*L,* 67).

It was 1904, Maugham was thirty, and he felt himself in a rut, needing the stimulation of travel for the sake of his work. He went to Paris, where his study of individuals intensified. Returning to London, changed as traveling always did for him, he wrote *The Magician,* based on Aleister Crowley's life, an individual he had met in Paris. And many of the people he had studied there would serve as models for his characters. France thereafter would represent to him freedom; and always England would represent restriction.

In London at a party in 1906 Maugham met "the one female love of his life": Ethelwyn Sylvia Jones, called "Sue," the daughter of Henry Arthur Jones, the popular dramatist who had praised his first novel. She was twenty, he was thirty-two. She had, Maugham states, "pale golden hair and blue eyes; except that she was less florid and less buxom, she reminded one of Renoir's luscious nudes. She had a lovely figure, but her chief grace was her smile. She had the most beautiful smile I had ever seen on a human being." He became her lover. On the way home that evening she asked him how long their affair would last. Maugham speculated, "Six weeks." It lasted eight years (*L,* 67). She would be the model for Rosie in *Cakes and Ale* (1930).

Theatrical Success

Having had no measure of success in the theater—*A Man of Honour* in 1903, for instance, ran only one night—Maugham was delighted when in 1907 his play *Lady Frederick* began a successful run. With this play he launched an "uninterrupted twenty-six year career as a dramatist, during which he had twenty-nine plays produced." The play ran for over a year. Maugham wrote: "Its success meant much to me. During my ten years as a professional author I had never earned more than a hundred a year and those thousand pounds my father left me had gradually dwindled to next door to nothing" (*L,* 110). In 1908 he had four plays running in London at once: *Lady Frederick, Jack Straw, Mrs. Dot,* and *The Explorer.* He had reached his goal. He was the successful dramatist that he aimed to be and that the dramatist Henry Arthur Jones predicted he would be.

"Never stage-struck" and accepting fame as his due (*SU,* 102), Maugham refined his writing style to fit the reactions of his Edwardian audiences, increased his skill in comedy, and came more fully to understand the lessons of the French writers under whose influence he would spend his literary life. As Cyril Connolly observed in 1948, Maugham became the "champion of lucidity, euphony, simplicity, and the story with a beginning, a middle and an end, the doctrines of his French masters."[59] In his apprenticeship in playwriting from 1907 to 1913, from *Lady Frederick* (1907) through *The Land of Promise* (1913), Maugham learned his lesson: the importance of form, of conciseness, of simplicity, and a high respect for audience (an important consideration for the dramatist). These lessons would serve him well. And in his career, Maugham would earn the reputation of being "the most resolute and coherent of the opponents of fine writing."[60] This style he felt was in keeping with the times: "For my part I prefer plain writing and I think it is more in the spirit of our day. But to write plainly is not a gift of nature: it has to be learnt. Of course one must write in the manner of one's own period" (*WPV*, 22).

The Burden of Life

Although Maugham had the goal of achieving fame and fortune through his writing, once he attained these, he found them not enough. The misery of the past, his French beginnings, the burden of an unhappy childhood—all drove him back to fiction. Returning to his unpublished autobiographical novel and giving up play contracts for a while, he wrote steadily from 1911 to 1914. The result was what his critics and he himself considered his best work: *Of Human Bondage*, published in 1915.

In 1913, in the final stages of composing this novel, he decided to end the eight year affair with Sue Jones by marrying her. In Chicago in the fall of that year, he proposed marriage to her. Unbelievably, and totally unexpectedly, she declined his offer. And in December of the same year, she married Angus McDonnell, the second son of the sixth earl of Antrim. Sue Jones, a minor actress, had rejected Somerset Maugham, the famous writer.

Within a few months, in 1914, he met again and began seeing Syrie Wellcome, the unhappily married daughter of a famous English philanthropist, Dr. Thomas Barnardo. Soon it was known throughout London that he was her lover.[61] Maugham was forty. If he meant to marry and have children, it was time. But, it was "the condition" that appealed to him. He wrote: "It seemed a necessary motif in the pattern of life that I had designed, and to my ingenuous fancy . . . it offered peace; . . . I sought freedom and thought I could find it in marriage" (*L*, 190). Of course, such a marriage would also serve as the perfect cover for his homosexual inclinations. While still at work on *Of Human Bondage*, he turned his wishes into fiction and drew the type of marriage that he wished for—in the character of Sally, the woman Philip is soon to marry, at the end of the novel.

The next year, 1915, Syrie gave birth to their only child, a daughter, Liza. It would be two years, however, before they were married, 1917. The marriage was to be an unhappy one, ending finally in divorce in 1929.[62]

Productivity and Change

The period from 1915 to 1930 was perhaps the most important one in Maugham's long literary career. During this time he published plays, short stories, travel books, and novels—all with large reading audiences—many of which will serve, no doubt, as a measure of his contribution to modern literature. Three of his best-known plays— *The Circle* (1921), *Our Betters* (1923), and *The Constant Wife* (1927)— were successfully produced during this time. In addition, he published *The Trembling of a Leaf* (1921), his first short-story collection since the 1898 *Orientations* volume. His second and third travel books, *On a Chinese Screen* (1922) and *The Gentleman in the Parlour* (1929), were also published. Besides his autobiographical *Of Human Bondage* (1915), he produced three other important novels: *The Moon and Sixpence* (1919), *The Painted Veil* (1925), and *Cakes and Ale* (1930).

Several shaping influences date to this period in his life. In 1917, he was married. In 1915, he was serving England in its war effort (entering in 1914: first in the ambulance service—where he met Gerald Haxton—the "male love of his life").[63] Later he served as an intelligence agent in Switzerland and then in Russia, traveling extensively. These experiences as a spy, like many of the other observations and events of his life, would find their way into his writings. *Ashenden*, a collection of short stories published in 1927, was the happy outcome of these war years in the service of his country. In 1916, while on a voyage with Gerald from San Francisco to Honolulu, he met Bertram Alanson, a Jewish-American stockbroker and later president of the San Francisco Stock Exchange. They became fast friends. In the early 1920s Alanson would begin the lifelong task of investing Maugham's money—handling it so wisely that Maugham would become incredibly wealthy. Returning in 1917 from his Russian mission ill with tuberculosis, Maugham would recover in a sanatorium in Scotland and, while regaining his health, manage to keep up his writing.

Throughout the 1920s Maugham was recognized for his witty—if cynical—novels and short stories and for his well-constructed plays—works that never failed to entertain. His plays were highly successful. *The Circle* (written in 1919) was produced in 1921 and enjoyed a successful run in London (181 performances). In 1926 and 1927 *The Constant Wife* played in New York (295 performances) and London (70 performances). In 1927 *The Letter,* Maugham's "first and only thriller," met with enthusiastic audiences—338 performances in London.[64] Following his second collection of short stories with two other collections—*The Casuarina Tree* (1926), based on his Malaysian experiences, and *Ashenden,* an account of his World War I spy activities—Maugham was able to interest a wide range of readers. And throughout this productive period of his life, his travels continued—not just between London, New York, and Paris—but throughout the world, giving him stimulus and inspiration. Maugham wrote: "I came back from each of my journeys a little different. In my youth I had read a great deal. In contact with all these strange people I lost the smoothness that I had acquired when leading the humdrum life of a man of letters, I was one of the stones in the bag. I got back my jagged edges. I was at last myself" (*SU,* 202).

But the crown of this period of unbelievably productive literary effort was *Cakes and Ale.* Although its publication was greeted with cries of slander—claims that Driffield represented Hardy who had recently died and that Alroy Kear was clearly based on Hugh Walpole, a popular writer of the day—it was quickly recognized as a major work. As in *Of Human Bondage* Maugham had found a place to use a personal experience that carried emotional importance for him; there was place here for the female love of his life—Sue Jones as Rosie.

Completion and Assessment

The 1930s proved to be an equally productive period in the career of this writer. His reputation continued at a high level. However, toward the end of the decade he found himself assessing the contribution he had made to literature. Critics acknowledged his output and the craftmanship of his writing, but found him weak in many ways. Maugham wrote: "In my twenties the critics said I was brutal, in my thirties they said I was flippant, in my forties they said I was cynical, in my fifties they said I was competent, and now in my sixties they say I am superficial" (*SU,* 219). It was more than his not reaching again the high artistic achievement of *Of Human Bondage*. In 1939 he was sixty-four years old. He felt that the pattern was completed, the house built. But despite the anxiety that his questionable position in English literature may have caused him, he believed above all that it was natural for an author to desire to be read by as wide a circle of readers as possible. And he now had a large audience. After his last play, *Sheppey*, produced in 1933, Maugham turned exclusively to fiction. He published three quality novels: *The Narrow Corner* (1932), *Theatre* (1937), and *Christmas Holiday* (1939). He also published two important collections of short stories: *Ah King* (1933) and *Cosmopolitans* (1936). He did publish one travel book, *Don Fernando* (1935). Venturing once more into personal revelation, the first direct attempt since *Of Human Bondage* twenty-three years earlier, he published *The Summing Up* (1938), an autobiographical sketch—"not an autobiography"; "no one can tell the whole truth," he wrote (*SU*, 1, 10). It is in these two remarkable works of autobiographical revelation that Maugham attempts to anticipate critics and does address and plead, however indirectly, for his rightful position in literature.

Several critical assessments began to appear in the 1930s: Richard Heron Ward's and Richard A. Cordell's in 1937. Frank Swinnerton, in *The Georgian Scene* (1939), proclaims: "He was not an innovator, moral or technical." Swinnerton does observe, however, that "where Shaw, Galsworthy, and Wells concerned themselves with society, and directed attention to faults in its structure, Mr. Maugham's exceptionally keen eye was upon the follies of individuals."[65] Thus, in addition to recognizing Maugham's craftmanship, critics acknowledged his "keen eye" in perceiving the uniquenesses of individual behavior. In 1939, Richard Aldington wrote that Maugham "is accompanied by an ability to present . . . [his insights] in words; because he knows the arts of successful plotting and skillful narrative; and because he is a man of the world and not of the library."[66] But even here, Maugham has made a similar observation in *The Summing Up*, published the year before Aldington's statement: "I have gone into the world because I thought it was necessary in order to get the experience without which I could not write, but I have gone into it also because I wanted experience for its own sake" (*SU*, 88).

Fame and Anxiety: 1940–65

The 1940s were years in which Maugham was displaced because of the war; traveled throughout the United States; had numerous experiences that he, even at his advanced age, was able to make use of in his writings; returned to his villa after the war—and yet managed through it all to continue to produce. In contrast to many aging writers, such as E. M. Forster, Maugham never stopped writing, never yielded to the temptation of living on the considerable reputation he had already established with *Of Human Bondage* (1915), *The Circle* (1921), *Cakes and Ale* (1930), and *The Summing Up* (1938). Every morning he found his way to the writing table and managed to create new combinations of characters and events for his readers.

During this decade he wrote his last two short story collections, *The Mixture as Before* (1940) and *Creatures of Circumstances* (1947). Of the five novels that he published in this period, the most important is *The Razor's Edge* (1944), which was widely read by servicemen during the war and was shortly made into a movie. However, *Up at the Villa* (1941) and his last novel, *Catalina* (1948), deserve to be mentioned. In addition to these, Maugham published two collections of essays: *Books and You* (1940) and *Great Novelists and Their Novels* (1948).

The decade held much change for Maugham. It began with his escape from his French villa, the Villa Mauresque (which he had purchased in 1926), in the path of the invading German army. Making his way to the United States, by ship to England and by plane to New York, he was met at La Guardia Airport by Nelson Doubleday, his American publisher.

In the United States for the duration of the war, Maugham quickly adapted to the pace of life among the Americans, sensitive always to the impression that he and other Englishmen were making. He traveled often to see his good friends Bertram and Mabel Alanson in San Francisco. He spent time in Los Angeles, Chicago, and especially New York. Soon the cottage that the Doubledays were building for him on their South Carolina plantation was completed. This cottage with its peace and solitude became his base of operation while in the United States, a place to work, to rest, to entertain on a small scale, a place to which he could return.[67] He now took on speaking engagements, improved greatly from the agonies of the stammer, not only speaking for the war effort, which he often did, but also on literary and cultural topics. In the early forties, for instance, he visited Purdue University and met with a group of Richard Cordell's students. Several of his works were being produced as movies, notably, of course, *The Razor's Edge*, taking him to California for extended stays.

He corresponded with William Lyon Phelps of Yale University and even traveled to New Haven to make a speech. During this period, Maugham survived several tragic events: Robin, his nephew and a future writer, was wounded in the North African campaign and came to South Carolina to recover. Maugham's daughter would later divorce and remarry. Gerald Haxton, a companion since 1914, died of tuberculosis in 1944, a severe blow to the aging Maugham. But throughout all these changing events and disturbances in his life, Maugham continued as always to find each morning that magic in the composing process. He continued to produce writing that interested readers.

In 1946, as the war was coming to an end, Maugham decided to donate the manuscripts of "The Artistic Temperament of Stephen Carey" and *Of Human Bondage* to the Library of Congress. The ceremony on the day of the presentation in Washington was elaborate, with several speeches, the featured one by Maugham on the composition of these two works. It is interesting to note that on the day when Maugham was thus being celebrated and honored, Sue Jones, the female love of his life, Rosie of *Cakes and Ale,* was living in this same capital city.[68] He may have longed to do as Ashenden did in that 1930 novel: go to the aging former love and ask what she ever saw in the man for whom she rejected him. No doubt she would have said, as Rosie did, "He was always such a perfect gentleman." Not long after the ceremony ended, Maugham was on his way by ship to the Villa Mauresque which he would find severely damaged by the six years of war.

Taking time out only to restore the villa, Maugham soon returned to his writing table. Before the decade ended, he published *Catalina,* his last novel (1948); *Great Novelists and Their Novels* (1948), a collection of essays; and a *Writer's Notebook* (1949), his own notebook, which he had kept since 1892. Now in his mid-seventies, Maugham resumed his normal work schedule: four hours of work each morning followed by relaxation and entertainment in the afternoon and evening.

In the 1950s Maugham was truly a celebrity. He was perhaps, as Martin Day observed in 1965, the most widely read English novelist of the twentieth century.[69] Ted Morgan even suggests that Maugham, in many ways, is to the twentieth century what Charles Dickens was to the nineteenth.[70] In his last years, he lived the life of the Grand Old Man of Literature. The villa was a favorite stopping spot for the famous: Winston Churchill, Grace Kelly, Adlai Stevenson, Ian Fleming. Movies were made of more of his works and his short stories were on the BBC. *Of Human Bondage* was again made into a movie with Laurence Harvey as Philip and Kim Novak as Mildred.

Maugham was named Companion of Honour, had an audience with Queen Elizabeth, ate at the Garrick Club, and spoke at the Royal Academy. In 1953, he was invited to have dinner at the Royal Academy and to make a short speech. His friend Gerald Kelly was then serving as president and asked Queen Elizabeth if she would sit by Maugham. At first she was fearful but, with Kelly's assurance that Maugham could be the best of company, she agreed. The evening was a success, and when the queen learned that Maugham had come all the way from France to sit next to her, she thought that the greatest compliment that had been paid her.[71] In the United States Klaus Jonas established the Center for Maugham Studies at Yale University—later moved to the University of Pittsburgh. Maugham spoke often: Columbia University, University of Heidelberg—to which he returned for the first time since his student days in the 1880s. They treated him, he wrote to his friend Bertram Alanson, like Rip Van Winkle. Continuing his travels, he was celebrated in grand style on his journey to Japan. On his eightieth birthday he was overwhelmed with attention: letters, telegrams, flowers, visitors. Publications of appreciation, interviews, assessments appeared in all the leading magazines, and Klaus Jonas published *The Maugham Enigma,* a collection of essays about Maugham's career.[72] Yet, as always, Maugham did not stop writing. He published two collections of perceptive and well-written essays during this decade: *The Vagrant Mood* (1952) and *Points of View* (1958).

The last years of the decade and those of the sixties—until his death in 1965—were not happy ones for Maugham. The pattern he had designed for his life was complete, and although signs of the end were evident, life continued. In 1958, the last of the friends from his own generation, Bertram Alanson, died suddenly. Maugham had outlived them all. Karl Pfeiffer published his damaging book—adding to the negative critical image that Edmund Wilson had made so forcefully in 1947. In 1959, Maugham's mind began to slip. His behavior was erratic and difficult for Searle to handle. He burned many of his manuscripts and letters.[73] Maugham put a notice in the *Times* that all of his letters should be returned to him. He attempted to adopt Alan Searle, his male companion. His daughter successfully challenged Maugham in court over the sale of paintings that he had earlier given to her. In print, in "Looking Back" (1962), he wrote derogatorily of Syrie, his former wife, dead since 1956.

But to the very end, he wrote. In addition to the fascinating "Looking Back," Maugham published *Purely for My Pleasure,* an account of how he acquired his art collection. Both of these works are remarkably well written. To the last Maugham's prose is clear, simple, natural. His legacy: writing must never obscure its meaning, must never fail to interest, to entertain.

Chapter Two
Pattern of Life
Style of Life and Work

Although the relationship between Maugham and his readers took him ten years to establish (1897–1907, from the publication of *Liza of Lambeth,* his first novel, to the performance of *Lady Frederick,* his first successful play), once begun, it deepened and intensified over the next fifty-five years during his lifetime. And even today, it continues in television productions of his plays and short stories, dramatized versions of his novels, and revivals of his plays in London and New York, as well as through the many copies of his works sold and read each year—many of which are still being issued in new editions (*Of Human Bondage,* published first in 1915, has never gone out of print).

Readers are drawn to the Maugham persona—the "I" of his first person narratives, the external narrator, the Maughamian character of his stories—never central, but always balancing the comments, actions, attitudes of the other characters, and always influencing the reader's involvement. Maugham, the often elusive author behind the writing, puzzles readers. He has always been observed with considerable interest, occasionally with contempt, often with bewilderment.

As well as being a writer—dramatist, novelist, short-story writer, editor, essayist, autobiographer—Maugham was, as has been observed above, a man of the world, a medical student at London's St. Thomas's Medical School, earning the M.D. degree, but never practicing after receiving it; an obstetric clerk to St. Thomas's out-patients, mostly from the nearby Lambeth slums, who brought sixty-three children into the world (*SU,* 8); a World War I British intelligence agent; the chief agent in Russia for the American and English secret service in 1917; a world traveler; a companion and lover of Gerald Haxton and Alan Searle; brother of Frederick Maugham, lord chancellor of England; uncle of the novelist Robin Maugham; husband of Syrie Wellcome; a father who attempted to disinherit his daughter Liza. Although this impressive list of relationships and roles implies a very active participation in life, Maugham was essentially always an outsider, more passive than active, living—as he often said—through the characters of his invention.

Very early Maugham himself sensed that he was different from others. Certainly the circumstances of his life—his French childhood, his stammer, the death of his mother and then of his father, poor health, unhappy school experiences, difficulty in finding a suitable profession—contributed to the sense of uniqueness that he felt. And even his natural temperament, what he termed "artistic" in "The Artistic Temperament of Stephen Carey," led him to a keen awareness of his separateness. He was not usual, he felt. He came to see himself as an outsider.

Maugham saw his life as an art work: having a pattern, with a beginning, a middle, and an end. Consciously, he attempted to impose such an arrangement on his life. In 1938, in the autobiographical *The Summing Up,* Maugham first mentions that he had had such a plan from very early—"to design a pattern for my life . . . I wanted to make a pattern of my life in which writing would be an essential element, but which would include all the other activities proper to man, death would in the end round off in complete fulfilment" (*SU, 46, 49*). *The Summing Up* itself he saw as an important part of that plan: a summing up at the end of a normal life span; and "since I have put the whole of my life into my books much of what I have to say will naturally have found a place in them." With that book, Maugham felt he had "rounded off my life's work . . . completed in sufficient outline the pattern I set myself to make. . . . The house is built" (*SU, 9, 8, 285*). And in the 1962 "Looking Back" he states, "I had had for some time an idea, perhaps a foolish one, that I should like my complete production to have something in the nature of a pattern" (*L, 62*). But as early as 1927, eleven years before *The Summing Up* was published, in a letter to Paul Dottin ("the first critic to attempt a serious appraisal of Somerset Maugham's work":[1] in his *W. Somerset Maugham et ses Romans* [1928]), Maugham speaks of his life as a program, then carefully maps out the works he plans to complete in the next ten years—ending with a collection of essays summing up his life.[2] That final work was, of course, *The Summing Up,* and, as planned, all the works mentioned in this letter were completed in ten years, by 1937—although the autobiography did not see print until 1938.

The relationship between Maugham and his readers lasted some sixty-four years during his lifetime—beginning with his first novel,

Liza of Lambeth, in 1897 and his first published short story, "The Punctiliousness of Don Sebastian," in 1898, and ending with "Looking Back" in 1962. And it is this special relationship between Maugham and his reader that is so puzzling—a relationship that is centered in the Maugham persona—the presence of the wise, sensitive man of the world, confidant of the neglected and misunderstood individual, the world traveler; a cultured, well-read person who is always fascinated by the extremes in art, morality, life—by the aesthete and saint alike—but who ultimately must choose the practical, for in the end the concerns of ordinary life always dominate. And once established, the pattern of this unique relationship repeated itself, gaining in a cumulative power over the years.

Persona and Style of Life

Seen in terms of what psychologist Alfred Adler called *gemeinshafts-gehfuhl* or "social interest," the Maugham persona is not just a clever literary device that proved artistically effective and commercially profitable. It is rooted in and emanates from Maugham's own personality, the unique style of life that he fashioned for himself from the materials with which nature and circumstances supplied him.

The earliest memory was one of Adler's chief diagnostic aids, since "the fundamental estimate of the individual and his situation is contained in it; . . . it is his subjective starting point, the beginning of the autobiography he has made up for himself."[3] Whether this recollection is or is not the earliest in the individual's memory does not alter its usefulness in understanding the style of life: the individual's "choice . . . shows us that some interest or other must have attracted him to it . . . and thus gives a strong indication of his individual tendency."[4] It is this individual tendency that is the key to an understanding of Maugham.

The earliest recollection of Philip, the protagonist in Maugham's 1915 autobiographical novel, *Of Human Bondage,* is that of the security he felt with his mother. Waking Philip, the woman servant carries him to his mother's bed:

She stretched out her arms, and the child nestled by her side. He did not ask why he had been awakened. The woman kissed his eyes, and with thin small hands felt the warm body through his white flannel nightgown. She pressed him closer to herself. . . . The child . . . was very happy in the large, warm bed, with those soft arms about him. He tried to make himself smaller still as he cuddled against his mother, and he kissed her sleepily. In a moment he closed his eyes and was fast asleep.[5]

That memory frequently comes again to Philip. While at King's School, he often feels that life is a dream and that he will awaken to find himself in his mother's arms. And throughout his experiences at King's School, Philip is happy only when studying, which he finds much easier than other activities, and when resting in his bed evenings: "And often there recurred to him then that queer feeling that his life was nothing but a dream, and that he would awake in the morning in his own little bed in London" (*OHB*, 38).

If this memory is attributable to Maugham, then the description here is clearly of a condition of happiness and contentment in which he is small, quite passive, and receiving and enjoying comfort. He is *carried by* Emma, *kissed* by his mother, and *pressed closer* to her. He is very happy in the large, warm bed, with soft arms about him. His own activity is limited to making himself still more helpless, trying to make himself still smaller, cuddling against his mother. His only outwardly directed response is minimal in that he sleepily kissed his mother. This scene offers great solace to him and Philip remembers it often, especially when he is miserable. It is at these times also that life seems a dream and his role again is that of being passive. In Adlerian terms, the Philip-Maugham recollection would be an outstanding manifestation of "the pampered life style,"[6] that is, the life-style of a person who wants to be pampered.

With Maugham's position as the youngest in the family, his older brothers were a possible threat to his feeling of worth. According to Adler, "The youngest child has no followers but many pacemakers. He is always the baby of the family, probably the most pampered, and faces the difficulties of a pampered child . . . a youngest child may suffer from extreme inferiority feelings; everyone in the environment is older, stronger, and more experienced."[7] From this viewpoint, then, it is logical that Maugham would write: "I had always supposed that I should enter the law, but my three brothers, much older than I, were practicing it and there did not seem room for me too" (*OHB*, 40).

Style of Life Dramatized

In *Of Human Bondage,* Philip is presented as an only child, for which Maugham had artistic reasons. One obvious reason was sim-

plicity: to focus directly on the one child, and therefore more easily
and effectively show the security with his mother and the utter alone-
ness without her. Realizing that she had only a short time to live and
not wanting her children to forget her "utterly," Maugham's mother
had a photograph made of herself, a photograph which "always stood
on the little table" by his bed.[8] In the novel, "She could not bear to
think that he [Philip] would grow up and *forget, forget her utterly;* and
she had loved him so passionately, *because he was weakly and deformed,*
and because he was her child" (*OHB,* 13; my italics).

Beyond this artistic purpose of simplicity, the only child may represent a wish of Maugham, in the same way as does Sally, the woman
Philip is to marry at the end of the novel. Admitting that Sally represents a wish, Maugham writes later: "Turning my wishes into fiction . . . I drew a picture of the marriage I should have liked to
make" (*SU,* 122).

Concerning the only child, Adler explains: "His rival is not a
brother or sister; his feelings of competition are directed against his
father. An only child is pampered by his mother. She is afraid of losing him and wants to keep him under her attention. He develops a
'mother complex' . . . and wishes to push his father out of the family
picture."[9] In the novel both Maugham's elder brothers and his father
(who actually died after rather than before his mother) are literally
"pushed out of the family picture," that is, Philip is portrayed as an
only child and his mother as his only living parent.

The sense of inferiority that Adler maintains all humans share initially can often be intensified by and focused on organ inferiority. A
child inflicted with an inferior organ, according to Adler, is likely to
feel inadequately equipped for life's tasks and to feel the minus situation "more intensely than [does] . . . the average child." But, sig-
nificantly, the ultimate outcome of this "depends on the creative
power of the individual which expands outwardly according to no rule
except that the determining goal always is success," which depends
in turn upon "the individual's own interpretation of his position."[10]

Maugham, of course, suffered from stammering. In *Of Human Bondage,* he has Philip suffer from a clubfoot instead, and he has him
make use of this weakness as an aid in his movement from minus to
plus, his movement toward the goal of perfection.

After the loss of his mother and the consequent loss of the pam-
pering to which he was accustomed from her, as portrayed in his earliest memory, Philip suddenly finds his physical weakness and

imperfect organ, his clubfoot, useful in his relations with others. For instance, when Philip is preparing to leave for Blackstable after the death of his mother, he hears Miss Watkin and her sister talking to friends in the dining room. Knowing that he will be pitied, the nine-year-old boy (Maugham was ten at this point) went in:

There was a sudden hush . . . and Philip limped in.
"My poor child," said Miss Watkin opening her arms. She began to cry. . . . She could not speak.
After leaving the room, he waited on the landing to hear their conversation.
"Poor little boy, it's dreadful to think of him quite alone in the world. I see he limps."
"Yes, he's got a clubfoot. It was such a grief to his mother." (*OHB,* 4)

At first his deformity only allows him to feel painfully conspicuous, inadequate, to feel intensely inferior. But such feelings are increased by the ridicule of his school fellows. For instance, while playing a running game, Philip finds "his limp gave him no chance":

Then one of the boys had the brilliant idea of imitating Philip's clumsy run. Other boys saw it and began to laugh; then they all copied the first; and they ran round Philip, limping grotesquely, screaming in their treble voices with shrill laughter. . . . One of them tripped Philip up and he fell, heavily as he always fell, and cut his knee. . . . His heart beat so that he could hardly breathe, and he was more frightened than he had ever been in his life. . . . The boys ran round him, mimicking and laughing. . . . He was using all his strength to prevent himself from crying. (*OHB,* 33–34)

At another time when Singer and Philip are caught playing Nibs, a forbidden game, Philip does receive special treatment because of his clubfoot. The headmaster swishes Singer but, turning to Philip, says, "I can't hit a cripple" (*OHB,* 38).

However, Philip finds his sickly condition, his clubfoot, and his unfortunate family background also of some use in his relations to others, giving him power over them. For example, at one point a boy called Luard is playing with Philip's ebony pen-holder. He is warned that he might break it, and just at that moment, he does. Luard apologizes and offers to buy him another, but Philip says it had been given him by his mother before she died. Even though this is un-true—he had bought it himself—Philip cannot keep back the tears and feels as miserable as if it had been the truth.

In this connection Philip recalls a previous experience in which his weakness (in that case both the loss of his mother and his deformity) was used for a similar purpose—to create misery, and thus to gain a sense of power over others. That Philip was not aware of the "why" of his behavior is evident in this experience.

It should be added that although Philip is portrayed as unaware of the logic of his behavior, Maugham was both alert to this and understood Philip's goal and therefore much of his own life goal as he wrote the novel. Thus Philip comes to see the usefulness of his weak condition, of his unfortunate family situation, and of his clubfoot. These weaknesses offer at once an excuse for his aloofness and passivity, and a means of manipulating others, getting his way, and avoiding his sense of inferiority. It was no "accident of association" that guided his memory to select that scene with Emma and the Misses Watkin. Rather, it was the similarity of the experiences and the consistency of Philip's way of approaching life—his style of life.

At the age of sixty-four Maugham published the statement that although few writers achieve immortality through their works, any writer would consider it pleasant to think that "one may be read with interest by a few generations and find a place, however small, in the history of one's country's literature" (SU, 11). Of course, Maugham has been "read with interest" by several generations in not only his own country but in many countries and many languages, is still read with interest, and has a secure position in English literature. But of more importance is the fact that in this statement Maugham expresses "interest in the interest of others."[11] Clearly Maugham here sees the meaning of life as contribution to others.

Since "interest" involves "value" (i.e., one places value upon that in which he or she is interested), social interest serves as a "guiding cognitive structure by which decisions are made." In other words, "the function of social interest is to direct the striving toward the useful side."[12] By useful, Adler means "in the interest of mankind generally."[13] And ultimately it is this criterion of usefulness versus uselessness (i.e., the consequence of what the individual does, more than what the individual says) that is the most dependable measure of his social interest: "Since the value of any activity is to be judged by its usefulness to all mankind, whatever may have been included under social interest, self-actualization and growth, are also subject to this stipulation."[14] With this criterion, then, Adler allows even the highly unique individual his place in a creative, ideal society. By extending this concept of social interest into the future, one is able to see that the independent spirit not only has a place, but is the "ideally normal man." "The criterion of social usefulness, however, is applicable to nonconformity as it is to any other behavior. The question is whether the nonconformity is ultimately socially useful, in the interest of mankind, or valuable to mankind, or whether it is merely a rebelling for personal reasons."[15]

After viewing the self-interested young Maugham in the early Philip, one must wonder how, in what way, and at what point he gained this interest in others. The theme of the novel concerns Philip's quest for a philosophy of life, a meaning to life, a freedom from human bondage, or bondage to passion. Maugham took the title from Spinoza's *Ethics.* He was attracted to Spinoza's statement that experience is only valuable when through our imagination and reason we are able to turn it into foresight, thereby shaping our future and freeing ourselves from the past; submitting to passion is human bondage, exercising reason is human liberty.

With this theme Maugham invents characters whom Philip observes to be in one way or another bound by passion. Philip's helpless bondage to Mildred is the epitome of human bondage for this protagonist. His friend Cronshaw gives him a Persian carpet which he says holds the meaning of life, but each individual must perceive it himself. The climax of the novel comes in a moving scene with Philip in the British Museum. Immediately before, he has been told of a friend's death. Seated before some Athenian tombstones in the museum, Philip feels the influence of the place descend upon him. All the figures on the tombstones seem to be saying "farewell"—"that, and nothing more." It is then that he begins to question again the meaning of life, for which he has searched so long. Thinking of Cronshaw, Philip remembers the Persian rug that he had given him and Cronshaw's claim that it offered the meaning of life. Sitting there, Philip is suddenly struck by the conclusion, the answer to the puzzle: life has no meaning.

Although Maugham the person reports no experience so specific as this, he did reach the same reconciliation early in his life. In this quite existential resolution he found a purpose and meaning for life, a meaning in no meaning. His relations with others thereafter took on a special significance. No longer did he search aimlessly with the explicit purpose of expecting others to give him the meaning to life, but he now had an interest for the sake of giving meaning through his art, seeing now the meaning of life as contribution: "I have been attached, deeply attached, to few people; but I have been interested in men in general not for their own sakes, but for the sake of my work" (*SU,* 7–8).

This view is strikingly similar to that of Hans Vaihinger, a Kantian scholar at the University of Vienna, who influenced Adler: "It is senseless to question the meaning of the universe, and this is the idea expressed in Schiller's words: 'Know this, a mind sublime puts greatness into life, yet seeks it not therein.' "[16]

Any consideration of Maugham's social interest must therefore center around the contribution he made through his works—what he put into life. Throughout his life he remained somewhat aloof, introverted, and more of an observer than a participant. The areas of friendship and marriage were clearly subordinated to that of work. It was here that he gave most valuably. Although he used his handicaps as excuses for withdrawing, he did extend his own sensitivity to include others. Combining this and skill in writing, probably compensatory for his stammering, with his zest for working—consciously or unconsciously a striving to concretize his own worth as an individual—he succeeded in making a significant contribution to his fellow human beings.

Maugham, like most writers, was not fully aware, of course, of the contribution he was making through his writings. That is, his attention was upon his work—creating emotions, characters, plots that are faithful, harmonious, and plausible—less than upon the audience and any contribution he may have been making. Often serving as a critic, rather than a supporter of present-day society, Maugham held the weaknesses and shortcomings of society and individuals up for exposure, even ridicule, often for laughter. Occasionally he was even cynical, but stopped short of being a reformer. But the important point here is that his contribution was often one of finding weaknesses and faults in today's world. Above all, though, Maugham gave pleasure and entertained his audience. This, he maintained, was the highest purpose of art.

The Maugham persona certainly varies from work to work. And the dramatized narrator-persona of the first-person narratives becomes a compensation for him, as Calder observes: "a representation of the kind of person he would like to be."[17]

There is a striking similarity between the persona of the first published short story in 1898 and the persona of *The Razor's Edge,* published in 1944. And there is a striking similarity between the goals and values of the Maugham persona in all his works and the goals and values of Maugham, the writer—the man Somerset Maugham.

If the persona is only a literary mask, then it is such a mask, that, when removed, is found to be similar to the face. Essentially, the persona of *The Summing Up,* of the novels and short stories, as well as his letters—the guiding sympathy in the plays—are all rooted in the personality and life-style of Maugham. And the distinctive feature of this persona is its capacity for social interest.

Persona and Modern Readers

Exactly how the persona involves the reader, however, and what contribution Maugham makes to earn such an audience must be dealt with in some detail. An explanation of Maugham's own aim as a writer will help clarify this point. First of all, it must be remembered that Maugham's watchwords were *simplicity, lucidity,* and *euphony*—in that order; that his models were from the Augustan Age and neoclassical period—Dryden, Swift, Voltaire; and that he admired Maupassant and Kipling for their sense of form, order, and simplicity. Second, it must be remembered that Maugham is a comic dramatist, not a poet—by his own admission: "I have small power of imagination. . . . I have been incapable of those great, sustained flights that carry the author on broad pinions into a celestial sphere. My fancy, never very strong, has been hampered by my sense of probability. I have painted easel pictures, not frescoes" (*SU,* 81).

In Charles Henry Hawtrey's memoir, *The Truth At Last* (1924), Maugham writes an introduction praising this famous comic actor for his art in acting. What he says of Hawtrey's acting art could be said as well of Maugham's storytelling and playwriting art: "[he] added as much as he received and often much more. He built up a part, giving it a life of its own, and adding to it his own vitality, good humor and charm."[18] Maugham, too, served his apprenticeship in the London theaters: learning the importance of form, economy of expression, and dialogue.

In the same introduction Maugham further praises Hawtrey for the naturalness of his acting. He observes that "the public worshipped him, but somewhat ignorantly, for his naturalness deceived them into thinking that there was little more in his acting than charm and ease." Then, as Maugham tells of the art of Hawtrey's naturalness,

Maugham could very well be speaking of his own simplicity, lucidity, euphony:

The natural actor is as far from the naked truth of fact as the ranting barnstormer. No one could say a line with the naturalness of Charles Hawtrey, so that when you heard him you said, "He speaks exactly as though he were in a drawing-room, it is not acting at all"; and yet it was acting all the time, art and not nature, the result of his instinctive sense for the stage and his experience; and the line was said not as it would have been said in a drawing-room but as it needed to be said in order to get over the footlights.

Finally, Maugham says of Hawtrey: "He had a just, perhaps even an exaggerated, sense of his limitations; but within his scope he exercised more originality of invention and a greater variety of humorous observation than the public, with its strangely incomplete appreciation of acting, gave him credit for."[19] Again here Maugham could be speaking of his own contribution.

But certainly Maugham ran the same risk as Hawtrey—choosing the low, more subtle style in a day when the applause went to the grand style. He knew himself well and he knew, for instance, that "Macaulay and Carlyle were in their different ways arresting; but at the heavy cost of naturalness. Their flashy effects distract the mind. They destroy their persuasiveness; you would not believe a man was very intent on ploughing a furrow if he carried a hoop with him and jumped through it at every other step. A good style should show no sign of effort" (*SU*, 42). And Maugham knew that the grand style would bring greater applause: "It is obvious that the grand style is more striking than the plain. Indeed many people think that a style that does not attract notice is not style. They will admire Walter Pater's but will read an essay by Matthew Arnold without giving a moment's attention to the elegance, distinction and sobriety with which he set down what he had to say" (*SU*, 35).

The risk, of course, is that, as in the cases of Hawtrey and Arnold, his art will be missed—but not the consequence of that art. The legacy of Somerset Maugham is simply that he is read and enjoyed, that his naturalness entertains. One is reminded of Gilbert Highet's description of how easily we forget the contributions of our teachers—especially the skillful, subtle tutors: they become "an example and a friend." They do not "overpower . . . or convert" a student into a "carbon copy." To avoid this they play down their "own originality" and refrain from turning on their full power. They are "flexible and changeable" rather than appearing "bold" and "strong." But this very "self-forgetfulness," which makes them good teachers, "very often causes us" to forget them, "sometimes even prevents" us from "realizing how much" we owe them.[20]

Similarly, Maugham's contribution is at once simple and complex. He may not dazzle us with poetic flights of imagination, but, as Richard Cordell states, he "quickens our understanding of man, our tolerance for his weaknesses, our amused awareness of his pretenses, a sympathy for his ineptitude."[21]

Chapter Three
Early Apprenticeship

An Overview

Believing that the artist "can within certain limits make what he likes of his life," that only he "and maybe the criminal" can make his own pattern of life, Maugham was "ambitious to make a name" for himself as a writer (*SU,* 34, 79). In 1892, from the very first of his life in London and even though in medical school, he set out to become a writer. Belief in personal freedom and the need for financial success were deep-seated motivations for Maugham, then and throughout his life. "Personal freedom has been one of his absolutes, both in instinct and intellect, good in itself; and at a tender age he learned the secret of it, the key to it, was financial independence,"[1] wrote Glenway Wescott, a friend and fellow writer—a statement published in 1964, the year before Maugham's death. And fame and fortune did come to Maugham after a period of apprenticeship: first in fiction, and then in the theater.

During the first period of Maugham's development, 1897–1907, he was trying his hand at several types of writing—the novel (naturalistic, historical, gothic novel), drama (first somber and serious, then comical), nonfiction (the essay, travel literature), short story, even journal editing (the short-lived journal the *Venture*), and article writing—but not reviewing.[2] Also, he was searching for a style that suited his purposes and that appealed to the audiences of the day, working through the influence of the Victorian aesthetes (whose current popularity undoubtedly tempted and pressured him) and that of the French writers (whom he admired and with whom he instinctively agreed). And he was experimenting with specific matters of tone and technique: searching for a stance, a persona, and a way of relating to the audience—serious or humorous, direct or indirect, formal or informal, etc. It was a time of learning for Maugham.

In the second period, 1908–1915, Maugham had found a way of relating to the audience, had found a style that he believed in and that was well received by Edwardian audiences, at least in the theater. In fiction he had had less success. And yet, if we can believe his stated purpose, he had already achieved the goal he set for himself: to write two or three novels in order to establish a reputation, so that theater managers would take him seriously. And he was definitely taken seriously now. As John Russell Taylor states: "Maugham [in 1908] took the London theatre by storm."[3]

But his novels were not unsuccessful. Perhaps Maugham realized that novels and short stories would touch a wider audience than plays, would give him greater permanence, and would be considered serious literature in a way that his comedies never could—at least as drama was then considered.[4] After six years of apprenticeship in the theater, Maugham, refusing all play contracts, turned once more to the autobiographical novel, a genre much in vogue with contemporary readers—in the bildungsroman tradition of Goethe's *Wilhelm Meister* (1821–29), having most recently been taken up by Samuel Butler in *The Way of All Flesh* (1903). Reworking the material of his life—from memory, he maintained—Maugham drew upon his theatrical experience and upon his lessons in form and style. This time—for he was making use of the same experiences of "The Artistic Temperament of Stephen Carey"—he knew his material well, had lived the lives of the characters, and had dug deeply into the memories of his unhappy childhood and his lifelong searches, unsuccessful as they were, for love, for God, for meaning. *Of Human Bondage* appeared in 1915. Although receiving mixed reviews in a world then troubled by war, it has enjoyed a growing success—and has never been out of print since its publication. Maugham's reputation was finally established.

Beginning of a Career

While still a student at St. Thomas's Hospital, Maugham published *Liza of Lambeth* with Fisher Unwin of London. A naturalistic novel in the tradition of the slum fiction of George Gissing and Arthur Morrison, it was based largely upon Maugham's own observations while serving as an obstetric clerk in the London slums of Lambeth.

Liza of Lambeth is a remarkable first novel. It reveals Maugham's economy of style: saying all that is needed for understanding, but no more. It displays his skill at dialogue, clever character delineation, well controlled tone, and functional dramatic structure. Richard Heron Ward, one of Maugham's early critics, maintains that Maugham wrote the novel because he was so "deeply impressed with the suffering, both spiritual and physical, of the poor . . ." whom he saw in Lambeth.[5] And yet Maugham chose to write in the impersonal manner of Flaubert. Richard A. Cordell, the leading American Maugham critic since the thirties, calls it "dry and cold . . . baldly objective [but] . . . a brilliant work of reportage, free of superfluous detail and comment . . . unvarnished account . . . a period piece with current grotesque slang of the cockney, the amazing costumes and coiffure . . . , the innocent vulgarities of a Bank Holiday in the eighteen nineties . . . as vital as a drawing by Hogarth."[6] But even with this characteristic objectivity and detachment, there is an unmistakable attitude, a persona. As Raphael observes, "the simplicity of the story and the detachment with which it is put down do not conceal a measure of indignation and pity."[7]

Maugham's notebook entries from this period—not published until 1949—offer further evidence of his being struck by the hopes, the sufferings, and the risks of the patients that St. Thomas's Hospital cared for. In one entry, dated 1897, Maugham tells of witnessing a cesarean, at that time a new and dangerous operation, on a woman who had been unable, despite several pregnancies, to have a child. She and her husband had wanted one badly enough to take the chance. The operation seemed to go well. "This morning," Maugham writes, "I was in the ward and asked one of the nurses how she [the patient] was getting on. She told me she'd died in the night. I don't know why, it gave me a shock and I had to frown because I was afraid I was going to cry." Even though he did not know her, he was moved by the passion she had "to have a baby, a passion so intense that she was willing to incur the frightful risk; it seemed hard, dreadfully hard that she had to die. . . . That poor woman."[8]

Moving from this entry—which was actually written the same year that the novel was published, 1897—to a page of *Liza of Lambeth,* one can easily detect the similarity of the observer/narrator—objective and detached, yet sympathetic and concerned for the plight of the poor and sick: "Worst off of all were the very young children, for there had been no rain for weeks, and the street was as dry and clean as a covered court, and, in the lack of mud to wallow in, they sat about the road. . . . The number of babies was prodigious; they sprawled about their mother's skirts."[9]

In this novel Maugham establishes a style of clarity, simplicity, and naturalness—a style that became his trademark. From the very first of his career, the act of writing came easily to him: "to write was," Maugham stated, "an instinct that seemed as natural as to breathe. . . ." It was only later that he became aware of the fact that his "language was commonplace, my vocabulary limited, my grammar shaky and my phrases hackneyed." Perhaps, he speculated, writing had come so easily for him that he never stopped "to consider if he wrote well or badly" (*SU*, 22–23).

Beyond these dramatic characteristics, though, the critical reader will note Maugham's skillful structuring of the story, designing it as if he were writing a play, not a novel. The entire work, in fact, can be viewed in three parts: a beginning, a middle, and an end; or act 1, act 2, and act 3, or in the four-part dramatic structure of exposition, complication, reversal, and denouement. In the first act (chapters 1 through 4), Maugham introduces the main characters: Liza, an exuberant, unmarried eighteen-year-old youth who lives alone with her mother; Jim, the married, new man in Lambeth, with whom Liza falls passionately in love; Tom, an unmarried youth who is helplessly and hopelessly in love with Liza, condemned to watch Liza's involvement with Jim deepen (the exposition). But as one would expect, there is more in this first act than the introduction of the characters and the major conflicts (beginning of the complication). The setting, the atmosphere, the tone all are presented with clarity and simplicity. Moreover, the first act prepares the audience for the act to follow: Liza's early passion for Jim; Jim's attraction to Liza; Tom's sense of rejection; the community itself and its code: celebrating with Liza, tolerating individuals with diverse personalities and varying degrees of self-interest: Liza, Jim, Tom, Mrs. Blakeston (Jim's jealous, irate wife), Mrs. Kemp (Liza's selfish, drunken mother)—and punishing those who deviate from its code. The activities and relationships that must be developed are set out clearly in this first act: the bank holiday, the relationship of Liza and Jim, Liza and Tom, the relationship of Sally and Harry, Liza and her mother, Jim and his wife. Then in act 2 (chapters 5 through 8), the middle part, these expectations are fulfilled: the bank holiday is successfully festive, the passion and attraction of Liza and Jim for each other intensify, Liza and Tom drift further apart, and the tension mounts between Liza and her mother and especially between Jim and his wife (the complication continues). By developing these expectations a step further, Maugham heightens the anticipation of the reader to know how these conflicts and difficulties can, and how they will, ultimately resolve themselves. Finally, in act 3 (chapters 9 through 12), the end of the story, these anticipations are satisfied.

Chapter 9 opens at the height of Liza and Jim's happiness. Shortly, though, problems develop—foreshadowed by the loss of happiness in Sally and Harry's marriage—Liza, now pregnant, is confronted in the open street by the stronger and larger Mrs. Blakeston, Jim's wife, angry and revengeful (the reversal). The consequences quickly follow. They fight. Liza loses, has a miscarriage, and dies (the denouement). This final act started with: "Thus began a time of love and joy. As soon as her work was over and she had finished tea, Liza would slip out and at some appointed time meet Jim" (*LOL,* 82). And it ends: "Jim turned away with a look of intense weariness on his face, and the two women began weeping silently. The darkness was sinking before the day, and a dim, grey light came through the window. The lamp spluttered out" (*LOL,* 137).

Within this dramatic structure, Maugham presents a story with considerable interest. It opens with a scene on Vere Street in London's Lambeth slums: hot, dry, oppressive. And because of the heat, almost everyone is out of doors. An Italian organ grinder rounds the corner. While everyone is aware that the young people have started up a dance, when Liza arrives, wearing a fresh new dress, radiating a distinct feminine vitality, and outdancing the others, all eyes are understandably on her alone. And as the scene closes, a chase develops: the young men running after Liza and, when she falls into the arms of Jim Blakeston, she is soundly kissed. It is from that one kiss, the reader senses, that tragic events will inevitably follow, events largely beyond the control of both Liza and Jim.

This opening scene reminds one of the beginnings of Thomas Hardy's *Tess of the D'Urbervilles,* published in 1892, a novel that Maugham read with enthusiasm.[10] In fact, even in this first chapter one notices a number of striking parallels between the two novels. First of all, the reader recognizes the similar vitality and innocence of the central female character: Liza and Tess. And there is a contagious joy and excitement about the individuals of the novels, particularly the young, and the mood of the community is captured at a festive moment. Also, both authors describe the setting with appropriate detail—thereby giving importance to the atmosphere. And in both novels there is a foreboding sense of inevitable doom as the early chapters close.

Liza's home represents one style of coping with the conditions in the Lambeth slums. Her stout, red-faced, widowed mother loves comfort—above everything and everyone in the world. Liza has her chores to keep up. And, in order for ends to meet, the family budget must be constantly supplemented with Liza's earnings. Having long ago learned to handle her mother with ease, Liza uses home as a sanctuary from the outside world, a world that constantly presses in on her with all of its excitement, opportunity, and risks. Home is where she can separate the appearances from the realities of her experiences, sort out the motives of her friends and acquaintances. Here she can dream of what her life will be and might be, and contemplate how it could have been and how it will all turn out.

In his relationship with Liza, the character Tom parallels that of Philip with Mildred in Maugham's *Of Human Bondage* (1915). He quickly senses his rejection as he and Liza both become increasingly aware of her irresistible passion for Jim. Tom, like Philip and Maugham himself, is an outsider, knowing little about common topics of boxing and sports, finding himself unable to join in the general banter of the conversation, remaining silent while others sing the popular songs of the day. The exciting bank holiday comes to a close as, riding home, Liza's waist is held by Tom and, unknown to Tom, her hand is held by Jim. The day ends with Jim kissing Liza goodnight.

The next morning at work, everyone feels the effects of the "previous day's debauch." Liza learns that Harry has proposed to Sally. A new play is being enacted at a neighboring theater, and those who have gone are urging the others to see it before it is over. Harry is taking Sally. Jim offers to take Liza, but she refuses. Jim, however, insists that he will wait for her outside on the final night. Predictably, Liza comes to the theater on that last night late—just to see if Jim has forgotten. He has not. They see the play together, and afterward they walk and talk, and both are aware of the passion that each has for the other.

"Come on," he said.
And together they slid down into the darkness of the passage. (*LOL,* 71).

If this were a novel by Thomas Hardy—such as *Tess of the D'Urbervilles*—the reader would expect the next chapter to be entitled "Maiden No More."

On Sunday morning, Mrs. Kemp, Liza's mother, sleeps late, giving Liza time to reflect on the activities of the previous night and time to play ball with the neighborhood children. She sees Tom, who now seems quite different to her. She sees Polly, Jim's daughter—who is Liza's age. And the same evening, she meets Jim.

These are the times of joy for Liza and Jim. Although people are quickly becoming aware of their relationship, Liza and Jim are conscious only of each other.

Their partings were never ending—each evening Jim refused to let her go from his arms, and tears stood in his eyes at the thought of the separation.

"I'd give somethin'," he would say, "if we could be together always."

"Never mind, old chap!" Liza would answer, herself half crying, "it can't be 'elped, so we must jolly well lump it." (*LOL,* 85).

Sally and Harry have a large church wedding. For all practical purposes, Tom has disappeared from Liza's life, and Liza envies Sally and Harry with their seemingly happy marriage. They seem to be the lucky ones. Not many weeks thereafter, though, Harry gets drunk and hits Sally:

" 'E was arright at first," said Sally.

"Yus, they're always arright at first! But to think it should 'ave come to this now, when they ain't been married three months, an' the first child not born yet! I think it's disgraceful." (*LOL,* 98)

But not long after this conversation Jim is drinking heavily and when he and Liza begin to quarrel, Jim hits her. They quickly make up:

"It wasn't the blow that 'urt me much, it was the way you was talking'."

"I didn't mean it, Liza." (*LOL,* 99)

For several days Liza's eye is black. And everyone knows what has happened.

Again, Liza is a friend to Sally. She talks to her about Harry, trying her best to cheer her up. In return, Sally befriends Liza by warning her of Mrs. Blakeston's intention to get even with Liza for being involved with Jim. And Liza is truly frightened of the bigger and stronger woman.

She meets Jim's wife in the open street with the entire community watching. No one dares interfere in such matters—except Jim, who comes too late. Liza has been too badly beaten to recover and we only learn of Liza's pregnancy toward the end—as complications result from the fight. She has a miscarriage and dies. No doubt, Maugham had witnessed similar tragedies in his work as an obstetrics clerk in Lambeth. In this novel he is uncompromisingly honest in portraying the plight of the central character. Maugham maintains the persona of the detached, objective narrator, presenting his account without comment or blame:

> Suddenly a sound was heard—a loud rattle. It was from the bed and rang through the room, piercing the stillness.
> The doctor opened one of Liza's eyes and touched it, then he laid on her breast the hand he had been holding, and drew the sheet over her head. (*LOL,* 136–37)

Liza of Lambeth created a storm, but was modestly successful. It was, in fact, not alone among those works that created storms, falling under the attack of a critical, often erratic, late Victorian audience. Such writers as Dante Gabriel Rossetti, George Meredith, and Thomas Hardy were similarly criticized for their frankness about sexual relationships and for their lack of optimism.

Furthermore, *Liza of Lambeth* fell squarely in line with the new morality of the last quarter of the nineteenth century; and, at the same time, just as squarely against the values of the early Victorians. Maugham was very fond of his brother Frederic's wife, and she greatly admired him. But his first novel, even though it was Maugham's work, was not in the least attractive to her. Years later her daughter explained quite simply that her mother after all was a "Victorian."[11] Perhaps Maugham's sister-in-law disagreed above all with the morality of the work, disagreed in the same way that she no doubt disagreed with "The Defense of Guenevere" and "The Haystack in the Floods" (William Morris), "The Blessed Damozel"[12] (Rossetti), and "Modern Love"[13] (Meredith)—or even *Tess of the D'Urbervilles* (Hardy). Liza, like the central characters of these works, yields ultimately to no absolute authority, maintains her dignity and integrity, and is true to herself and to her individual code of behavior—faithful, above all, to what and whom she loves and believes in.

In this novel, one can also see Maugham's interest in the theater. Liza and her friend Sally spend leisure moments imitating lives and manners from melodramas that they have seen. In the course of the novel, a play comes to town and everyone longs to see it. Maugham even describes the line of people outside the theater ("serpentlike string of people") waiting, and then its sudden surging into the theater: "At last a movement ran through the serpentlike string of people, sounds were heard behind the door, everyone closed up the men with women to keep close and hold tight; there was a great unbarring and unbolting, the doors were thrown open, and, like a bursting river, the people surged in" (*LOL,* 106). At the bank holiday a drama, *The Idyll of Corydon and Phyllis,* is presented, and at another point there is "much banter of a not particularly edifying kind respecting the garments which each person would like to remove"—which, the narrator adds, "showed that the innuendo of French fame is not so unknown to the upright, honest Englishman as might be supposed" (*LOL,* 59).

Maugham's narrative is detached and objective throughout: for, as Ward suggests, "he did not experience himself the suffering of the people in the slums of London: he could do no more, in almost all cases, than look on at it."[14] However, Maugham's sympathy and his presence are evident from the beginning. As Calder states, "Maugham's real concern is with the stifling and restricting nature of ghetto society. He views this life as an intensely tribal existence, with all of the pressures and unwritten laws which accompany it."[15] The story of this novel "is that of a strong individualist who attempts to defy the laws of the tribe and soon suffers punishment." If we consider the novel "a photograph of life in the slums," as Ward does,[16] then we must add that it is a photograph with a unique slant on reality, a distinctly Maughamian slant. In a statement published in the *Academy* the same year as the novel, Maugham admits that the reality the novel depicts is "sordid and nasty," but quickly adds that if the "book was to be written at all it has to be done truthfully."[17] He confesses that one of the reasons that he wrote it was to "induce" readers "to look a little less self-righteously at the poor, and even to pity their unhappiness." And it was that uniqueness that brought about what Maugham terms "the notoriety of *Liza of Lambeth*" (*SU,* 74).

There is, of course, one central character, Liza, who is essential to the meaning of this novel, as was Tess to Hardy's novel. The reader is struck by her vitality and exuberance from the first moment she appears. Calder says that Liza is "a character whose spirits are too strong and exuberant to be forced into the expected course of events."[18] Raphael maintains that "Liza's vitality is like that of a spring daisy which pushes between the hard slabs of a city pavement and then is crushed by unheeding boots."[19] As with Hardy's Tess, the narrator gives us a clear understanding of Liza's essential goodness, her purity, even her dreams and hopes for a life of fulfillment. And there is with both characters a sense of tragedy. Liza's downfall springs from her passion for Jim, a passion that binds her and alters her judgment. And, as with Tess, the basic selflessness and goodness of Liza's character is developed in contrast to her mother's selfishness, love of comfort, life of indulgence, and self-pity. No doubt this selfishness and hypocrisy were grounded in Maugham's own experience. His uncle, as portrayed in *Of Human Bondage,* thinks mainly of himself, his reputation, his comfort, his future, and his influence. He even takes trips and vacations without his wife. And if there is just enough food for one, then Maugham's uncle is accustomed to eating it—"to keep up his strength."

Maugham skillfully uses the environment to enhance the contrast between Liza and others, and to enlarge her character. Calder observes that the environment in this novel becomes "almost an entity in itself, with overwhelming power to influence events . . . the street is viewed as a trap, a force which plays a great part in the course of the action."[20]

And much of the action in the novel takes place out of doors. The basic narrative persona that Maugham chose "equipped him with a point of view suitable to a realistic novel." In his description of the environment Maugham effectively captures the claustrophobic narrowness of the slum and the ease and freedom the lovers feel when they emerge from it: "She walked close along the sides of the houses like a thief. . . ." Such use of environment is reminiscent of Fielding's character Tom Jones moving from the domain of Mr. Allworthy to the freedom and, as it turns out, precarious world beyond that environment. And of the outcome, the consequences, Calder observes: "In the final chapters of the novel, Maugham emphasizes the failure of Liza's attempt to defy Vere Street, and he displays the naturalist's belief in the effect of environment."[21]

One of the characteristics of this novel is its capacity to capture a sense of the community life with its "strong code of righteousness," "the feeling of the strength of the communal pressures in Lambeth." Some critics, such as Calder, maintain that the novel is essentially the "story of an individual's attempt to be free from the pressures to conform to the rules of a particular society." Whether or not one sees the work this way or as the tale of an individual becoming helplessly bound by passion, or even searching for meaning in a chaotic, contradictory world, it would be difficult to overestimate the importance of the "atmosphere of close communal living"—an atmosphere in which Maugham places Liza—whose "spirits are too strong and exuberant to be forced into the expected course of events."[22]

And the manner in which the reader is involved in this atmosphere and in this character is as unique and complex as the author himself. As Curtis observes, "the mature Maugham cultivated a friendly working relationship with his readers that became the constant feature of his work."[23] But this involvement is more complex than that statement implies. It is true that Maugham's persona is detached, aloof, objective, even clinical and unsentimental—a mere storyteller. As Raphael observes of this first novel: "A modern reader is unlikely to be shocked by *Liza of Lambeth*. The story is simple."[24] And much of that simplicity comes from the aloof and objective persona. Calder maintains that the "aloof character of the Maugham *persona*" owes its origin to Maugham's training and experience as a doctor—"to treat patients without causing an unbearable emotional strain on himself." This combined with "Maugham's natural reticence" gave him a "detachment which he retained throughout his career."[25]

But such qualities—aloofness, objectivity, reticence—would yield only a story told in a detached, unsentimental manner. There is more. The persona in Maugham's works skillfully and subtly involves his readers. In answer to a negative review of *Liza of Lambeth,* Maugham wrote (1897) that perhaps the reader (specifically the reviewer but a general reader as well) "will not entirely forget me; and the next time he is forced to go through some slums, he will not push aside with his umbrella the ragged child who is in his way, and when he sees a woman with a black eye, her face all pale and tear-stained he may not look upon her entirely with contempt."[26] And that is the unforgettable impression of the novel. But, unlike Thomas Hardy's narrator, who dogmatically drives home the points of his sermon after each experience of his heroine, Maugham characteristically maintains his detachment. And yet the reader has great sympathy for Liza. Ward deals with this paradox in Philip Carey, Maugham's character in *Of Human Bondage* (1915): he is always spoken of with compassion, yet this compassion comes from within the reader. "The secret is that Philip in the book . . . does not indulge in self-pity . . . he accepts, and acceptance of one's own suffering must bring tolerance toward it. . . ."[27] And of course this is also true with Liza. In *The Writer's Point of View*, Maugham spoke of the challenge that faces the writer: "the novelist is at the mercy of his bias. . . . However hard he tries to be impartial he cannot help taking sides. He loads his dice, sometimes knowing very well, and then he uses such skill as he has to prevent the reader from finding him out" (*WPV,* 13). And one such technique, one that Chaucer often employed in *The Canterbury Tales,* was to undercut the persona—to admit inadequacies, weakness, lack of understanding:

"Oh, I say," she said, "this is too bloomin' slow; it gives me the sick."

That is not precisely what she said, but it is impossible always to give the exact unexpurgated words of Liza and the other personages of the story; the reader is therefore entreated with his thoughts to piece out the necessary imperfections of the dialogue. (*LOL,* 7)

Thus, when we consider Maugham's dramatic involvement of the reader and the skillful and complex persona, we can understand why the novel attracted attention. Although it lacked the depth of characterization that his later works would have, it fulfilled in large measure what he later maintained a novel should have as its purpose— what a novel must have "in order to afford the reader with the intelligent pleasure he has the right to demand": "Let us consider for a moment what are the qualities of a novel. . . . It should have a coherent and probable story, a variety of plausible incidents, characters that are living and freshly observed and natural dialogue. It should be written in a style that is suited to the matter. If the novelist can do that he has done all that should be asked of him. His business is to please, not to instruct" (*WPV,* 12).

Little wonder, then, that a critic of the stature of Walter Allen would call *Liza of Lambeth* "the completest specimen of the naturalistic novel in English. . . . the novel remains remarkably fresh, and Liza still has her unquenchable vitality. Maugham is as detached as ever he has been, but the novel vibrates still with the passion of deeply felt observation."[28]

Experimentation

Considering new writing paths to follow after *Liza of Lambeth,* Maugham fell to the temptation of many young writers: to write beyond one's knowledge and experience, to seem to know and under-

stand more than one does. He was helped along this path by Andrew
Lang, a well-known critic of the day. In one of his articles Lang impressed Maugham with the argument that, since the young author
has so little experience in life, the only type of composition in which
such a writer can hope for success is historical writing. With such
material, Lang maintained, the writer would have "a story and characters" and "the romantic fervour of his young blood" would provide
the story with the necessary dash (*SU,* 162). Accordingly, Maugham
read works on medieval Italy in the British Museum to gain a sense
of that historical period. The result of these efforts was *The Making
of a Saint,* a story founded on Machiavelli's *History of Florence.* The
novel was "conceived in London"[29] and written in Capri during the
summer of 1897. It was written at "breakneck speed," according to
Morgan, and was "an exercise in historical reconstruction."[30] Looking
back in the 1930s on the composition of this work, Maugham wrote:
"such was my ardour that I had myself awakened every morning at
six and wrote with perseverance till hunger forced me to break off
and have breakfast. I had at least the sense to spend the rest of the
morning in the sea" (*SU,* 163). As he stated, "I had written my first
novel of what I knew, but now, seduced by this bad advice, set to
work on a historical romance" (*SU,* 163).

Thus, when *Liza of Lambeth* had such a success that Fisher Unwin
pressed him for a second novel, Maugham had one finished. Although
Unwin expected another slum novel, Maugham, having no more interest in the slums, sent him *The Making of a Saint.* Fisher Unwin
accepted it and brought it out in 1898 in a "First English edition"
and "Colonial edition" and in 1904 in a paper edition."[31] This novel
was also his first American publication—put out by L. C. Page of
Boston.

Maugham always considered it his worst novel and after these editions were published he would not allow it to stay in print.[32] His
attitude toward the novel and toward this experience, however, is remarkably positive. He states in *The Summing Up* (1938) that "even
the greatest authors have written a number of very poor books" (*SU,*
164). More importantly, in these statements Maugham admits much
of his early purpose in writing: for the most part the books he wrote
"during the first ten years after I became a professional writer [1897–
1907] were the exercises by which I sought to learn my business"
(SU, 165). Seen in this light, then, *The Making of a Saint* offers valuable insights into Maugham's years of apprenticeship.

The critical reception of *The Making of a Saint* was cool—at best. Although the *Spectator* reviewer praised it for "its life,"[33] the *Academy* captured the general reaction to Maugham's second novel by calling it "rather mediocre" and complaining that it "does not fulfill the expectations of *Liza of Lambeth*."[34] And the *Dial* found "nothing to indicate the 'making' in any psychological sense, of 'a saint.' . . ."[35] The *Athenaeum* also found the title "unintelligible."[36]

The clear, simple, natural style that had characterized *Liza of Lambeth* is not consistently present in *The Making of a Saint*. The *Bookman* reviewer recognized dramatic power in both novels: the "power which vitalized one is identical with the power that vitalized the other."[37] Although the dramatic power might be present in both, in *The Making of a Saint* it is never fully realized. As the reviewer of the *New York Evening Post Literary Review* stated, it is "sometimes a little awkward and sometimes a little boring."[38] Perhaps the most complete statement of the novel's failure to engage the audience in a dramatic manner was made by the *Literature* reviewer: "He [Maugham] makes his fifteenth-century Italians do the kind of things which such people actually did, but he does not succeed in convincing the reader that this was the way they did them."[39]

This lesson was a bitter one for Maugham, but one he learned well. If we can take his statements about why a play fails as having some relevance to the failure of a novel, then Maugham's statement in the 1939 edition of his collected plays is enlightening. A play fails, he states, for the following reasons: the "theme . . . does not interest," "poor characterization," "faulty construction," "verbose and heavy dialogue."[40] And in *The Summing Up* (1938), Maugham states: "I have never had much patience with the writers who claim from the reader an effort to understand their meaning." Such are the weaknesses of this second novel. Such lessons as these came to Maugham from the failure of *The Making of a Saint*.

The novel places demands upon the reader from the very first. It is set in fifteenth-century Italy and is introduced by a relative of the narrator, a narrator who has been a soldier of fortune and has since become a monk. The relative has a task not unlike that of the sympathetic editor of Herr Teufelsdröckh in Thomas Carlyle's *Sartor Resartus* (1833–34)—a work that Maugham had no doubt read: to sort through, select, and present the best of the prodigious and unorganized writings of an important individual. The story, then, consists of the memories of Filippo. He is part of a rather complicated con-

spiracy that finally ends with the assassination of the ruler of Forli.
But after taking over the city, the rebels are overpowered by outside
forces. The results are that many of them are brutally killed and the
others scattered. And in the end, of course, the narrator renounces
the world to become a monk—disillusioned not only by the fortunes
of war, but above all by the unfaithfulness of his lover Guilia
dall'Aste.

In his notebook entries—also written in Capri—for this period
(1896, the year before *The Making of a Saint* was published),
Maugham asks questions about morality, social change, and the
meaning of life—all subjects that find their way to a certain degree
into "The Artistic Temperament of Stephen Carey" and certainly into
Of Human Bondage, but not into *The Making of a Saint.*

But there are distinctive features of *The Making of a Saint* that
Maugham will exploit in later works. First of all, the use of a dramatized first-person narrator in the introduction is the early beginning of the Maugham persona/narrator. For instance, the narrator
begins by referring to a friend (actually Maugham) who has published
a controversial novel *(Liza of Lambeth).*[41] The persona obviously pre-
tends to agree with the critics—and naturally in the process of doing
so undercuts himself. The humor and irony of this situation are some
of the first in Maugham's writings. Also, the persona will make
concession to and confide in his clearly English readers: "I am painfully aware that the persons of this drama were not actuated by the
moral sentiments, which they might have acquired by education at a
really good English public school, but one may find excuse for them
in the recollection that their deeds took place four hundred years ago,
and that they were not wretched paupers, but persons of the very
highest rank" (*MS,* 14)

An equally important feature of this novel is the theme of bondage
to passion, seen in Filippo's hopeless passion for Guilia, a subject that
Maugham will develop in subsequent works. Woodburn O. Ross
maintains that there are three elements in this theme, elements that
are also developed in Maugham's *Mrs. Craddock* (1902): (1) a woman
(Guilia) appears one way but is quite different; (2) a man (Fillippo) in
the grips of a passion he cannot free himself from; and (3) the belief
that just knowing one's nature will not release one from the power of
passion.[42] Ross observes that in *Mrs. Craddock* Edward and Gerald
become Guilia, and Bertha becomes Filippo. Similarly Calder has observed that the "situation between the narrator and Guilia is an em-

bryonic version of the Philip-Mildred relationship in *Of Human Bondage.*"[43] Of course, as we have observed above, this same theme was present in *Liza of Lambeth.*

An Accomplished Novel

"Not unsuccessful" was Maugham's own evaluation of *Mrs. Craddock* (1902; *SU,* 164), his third novel. Critics, however have a higher opinion of this work. Calder considers it "the best that he produced until *Of Human Bondage.*"[44] Morgan calls it the "most fully realized of his works to date."[45] In 1920, E. Francis Edgett found it "as individual and original" as *Of Human Bondage* and *The Moon and Sixpence.*[46] Raphael even draws a parallel between Maugham's characters and those of D. H. Lawrence: "Edward Craddock appears to have those vigorous qualities which have come to be associated with Lawrentian gamekeepers . . . sexually attractive . . . coarse and stupid."[47] And in his 1955 preface to an edition of *Mrs. Craddock,* Maugham himself states that it provides "a faithful picture of life in a corner of England during the last years of the nineteenth century."[48]

For its day, *Mrs. Craddock* was considered "fairly daring." In fact, Maugham's publisher would not release it unless Maugham made certain changes—a common demand of late Victorian publishers.[49] As Calder has pointed out, "Bertha's passionate nature and her ruthless pursuit of Edward Craddock were examined with a frankness and thoroughness that shocked readers." Calder even suggests that the novel may well have influenced later writers and students of psychology. It "would not," he states, "be extravagant to claim for it [the novel's study of Bertha] a certain degree of influence on D. H. Lawrence and other later students of female psychology."[50]

The novel is set in Maugham's native Kent, near Whitstable, where he had lived with his aunt and uncle toward the end of the nineteenth century. Bertha Ley, a mature and sophisticated woman, falls in love with a farmer, Edward Craddock, a member of a class lower than her own. They marry in spite of the advice of her family. Her aunt, Miss Ley, looks on with understanding and tolerance, but with a degree of skepticism. However promising a mate Edward may have seemed before marriage, Bertha soon finds him insensitive to her and quite understandably they have less in common, less to share. Bertha becomes pregnant, but the child is stillborn. At this critical time in Bertha's life, Edward is unbelievably insensitive. And when shortly thereafter she visits Miss Ley in London, Bertha (now out of

love with Edward) falls passionately in love with Gerald Vaudrey, a
young boy she meets. But he does not love her. Life changes suddenly
for Bertha when shortly after her return home, Edward is killed in a
riding accident. Naturally, everyone feels sympathy for her. But the
reader shares Bertha's secret: her only feelings are relief and freedom.

The entries in Maugham's notebook for 1901, the year before *Mrs.
Craddock* was published, reveal a growing personal sense of skepticism
and unbelief, subjects that relate closely to the themes of the novel.
The following entries are typical:

Morality is the weapon which society in the struggle for existence uses in its
dealings with the individual. And all this effort of natural selection where-
fore? What is the good of all this sound activity beyond helping unessential
creatures to feed and propagate?

I'm glad I don't believe in God. When I look at the misery of the world
and its bitterness I think that no belief can be more ignoble. (*WN*, 63, 61)

In the many entries of this year, Maugham repeatedly takes up such
topics as the end of a life, belief in God, morality, duty, death,
Christianity, society, sin, religious systems, desires, hunger, ethics,
conscience, the dignity of man, love affairs (*WN*, 42–63).

As he had done in *Liza of Lambeth*, Maugham clearly based his
writing upon his own experience and understanding—a procedure he
had *not* followed in his second novel. Joseph Dobrinsky, the leading
French Maugham critic, detects this quality in *Mrs. Craddock*: the
novel, he states, transposes "with passionate veracity" a "painful
. . . experience of the author."[51] A. St. John Adcock in the *Bookman*
praised the portrait of Bertha: "subtle" and "masterly"; the minor
characters "cleverly drawn"; the social life of the Kentish countryside
"touched in with fidelity."[52] In a review of a 1928 edition of the
novel, the *Bookman* found the early Maugham more earnest, duller—
but the same. Perceptively, this reviewer understands the important
role that Miss Ley, the spinster aunt, plays in the work: "The chorus
of this disallowed tragedy, in the person of the heroine's spinster
aunt, a delightful cynical echo."[53] Failing to see this function, the
Athenaeum found her a disappointment "for she is announced as quite
a character."[54] Joseph Dobrinsky calls attention to the influence of the
French naturalists: it "testifies, both in the manner and in the matter,
to the influence of the French naturalistic school." He further praises
the "brilliance of the dialogue,"[55] as does Matti Paavilainen: "the
great merit lies in its witty dialogue."[56] Therefore, judging from the
critical reception and the assessment of literary critics, *Mrs. Craddock*

moves closer to Maugham's ideal of simplicity, naturalness, and clarity.

In this novel several themes appear that will become commonplace in Maugham's later writings. First of all, as mentioned above, there is the bondage of passion theme. Calder observes that Bertha's particular type and pattern of bondage—the woman "enslaved by her passionate nature, marries unwisely, discovers that her husband is dull, unresponsive and inadequate, and is finally freed from her intolerable bondage by his death"—will be developed in *The Painted Veil* (1925), *Theatre* (1937), and "The Human Element" (1930).[57] Raphael points to the importance of the theme of the "crass conformity of English provincial life."[58] And Morgan finds three thematic levels to the novel: (1) the study of the "stifling provincial society"; (2) the study of a woman who marries below her station; and (3) Maugham's personal working out of his own obsessions: mother endangered by pregnancy, a child stillborn, the pain of love, the quest of freedom, etc.[59]

Thus, the novel reaches a higher thematic and stylistic level than the earlier two novels considered in this study. Raymond Toole Stott, Maugham's lifelong bibliographer, states that in *"Mrs. Craddock* . . . for the first time one catches unexpected flashes of the later Maugham, with his worldly wisdom and uncanny intuitive understanding of human nature."[60] It is a novel in which, as Morgan states, "Maugham reveals himself through his characters."[61] Raphael pays high praise to Maugham's characterization of Miss Ley: "the detached raisonneuse whose persona is the first to have the Maughamian quality of detached worldliness that he was to wish in Willie Ashenden and finally in the character whom he called Mr. Maugham [in *The Razor's Edge*, 1944]."[62] And Calder calls attention to the closing of the novel (and specifically to Bertha's important affinity to her admired aunt, Miss Ley): "[*Mrs. Craddock*] ends with a pessimistic comment on the limitations of love and communication with others, but there is also a note of optimism for Bertha . . . [who] has achieved a kind of contentment in her freedom."[63]

In these three novels, then, and others he would write during the early part of his apprenticeship (1897–1907), Maugham had discovered many of his strengths and limitations. He no doubt had his sights on the goal of the career he had dreamed of: playwriting. And Maugham already had some hope of success. *Marriages Are Made in Heaven,* his first play, was performed in Germany under the title *Schiffbruechig,* for which Maugham made the translation. It ran for eight performances.[64] A one-act play, it revealed the influence that

Wilde, Pinero, and above all, Ibsen were having upon him. It was a beginning.

Maugham's treatment of the relationship between men and women in these three novels of preparation is noteworthy. In each he gives considerable attention to the imbalance in a relationship—whether the cause is money, class, or circumstances—the actual imbalance itself is the dominant impression that one has of the relationship; that is, its weakness, its imperfection. Conscious of his own imperfection, his stammer, Maugham came to view normality as an ideal. At first under the influence of his medical training, he saw this as true in human anatomy, but later in human relationships as well. In *The Summing Up* (1938), he gives an account of his experiences in the dissecting room at St. Thomas's Hospital: he had complained that a nerve he had been asked to identify was in the wrong place. The demonstrator explained that in "anatomy it was the normal that was uncommon," an explanation that Maugham never forgot. Of course, he was annoyed at first, but later he concluded: "it was true of man as of anatomy. The normal is what you find but rarely. The normal is an ideal." What most writers present, he came to see as a false picture: "they describe what is so exceptional that they seldom achieve the effect of life" (*SU, 67*). But Maugham not only portrays selfishness and vanity, shyness and laziness, etc., in *characters,* he depicts *relationships* that are equally marred.

In *Liza of Lambeth,* for example, Liza has an affair with a married man, whom she depends upon much more than he on her. Her vulnerability becomes more evident as the novel develops, and her downfall is inevitable—caught as she is in a conflict with the mores of society and circumstances reminiscent of Thomas Hardy—leaving nothing but disaster ahead of her. In *The Making of a Saint,* Filippo, a fifteenth-century Italian soldier, is disenchanted with the world largely because of the unfaithfulness of his lover, Giulia dall'Aste. Here again it is the one who cares the most who is ultimately the one victimized. And in *Mrs. Craddock* we are faced with a similar imbalance as Bertha is caught in a marriage to an insensitive, lower-class individual for whom she has had an entrapping bondage of passion. Ironically, her husband dies in a tragic accident at almost the very moment that she has freed herself from her bondage to him. And here, in the character of Miss Ley, Maugham makes his first use of a detached, critical observer.

Chapter Four
Later Apprenticeship

In the final period of preparation, 1907–15, Maugham had experiences and made decisions that influenced his future life and work. And for one of the first times in his career, he began to draw upon the emotions, dilemmas, and traumas of his present life for the material of his writings.

During this period Maugham had a series of love relationships—each creating its own unique anxieties—and establishing lifelong attitudes. He continued his affair, begun in 1906 in London, with Sue Jones, the female love of his life. It would not end, despite his humiliation at her unfaithfulness, until her rejection of his marriage proposal in Chicago in 1913. Also during this period, Maugham met Syrie Wellcome (1911) and began a love affair with her (in 1914). Their daughter was born in 1915 in Rome. He married Syrie in 1917 and divorced her in 1929. Finally, Maugham began a relationship in 1915 with Gerald Haxton, the male love of his life, a relationship that would end only with Haxton's death in 1944.

Having succeeded spectacularly with his comedies on the London and New York stages and having made a final break with the ornate and decorative style, Maugham continued to write plays. But he found himself drawn back to the writing of novels and to the autobiographical novel that he had begun some fifteen years earlier.

Theatrical Success

After several unpopular, rather somber plays, Maugham had the good fortune in 1907 of having *Lady Frederick* produced and having it succeed. He had, he later wrote, determined that the public wanted to laugh, to be thrilled—with sentiment. He knew that "if I had continued to write plays as bitter as *A Man of Honour* or as sardonic as *Loaves and Fishes* [his early plays] I should never have been given the opportunity of producing certain pieces to which not even the most severe have refused praise" (*SU,* 117). And he also determined to create an unusual female character, Lady Frederick, fit for a star. Set in Monte Carlo, the play portrays Lady Frederick as a widow with money problems. Eventually she rejects her much younger suitor and is rescued from financial ruin by her former suitor. Thus, marriage and the relationship between men and women—complicated by economic problems—are of central importance in this, his first successful play. It was the beginning of a twenty-six-year career as a dramatist and the first of twenty-five plays.

Written in what Sir John Ervine termed "the tradition of Congreve-Sheridan-Wilde . . . comedy of manners,"[1] the play opens with a mother, Lady Mereston, worried that her son, Charles, will propose to and marry Lady Frederick Berolles, a widow fifteen years his senior. She has sent for her brother, Paradine Fouldes, to help put an end to this possible marriage with Lady Frederick, with whom Paradine himself has once had a romance. Lady Frederick's brother, Captain Gerald O'Mara, who wishes to marry Rose, Admiral Carlisle's daughter, is also present. Lady Frederick does manage to persuade the Admiral that he should consent to this marriage. But her problem is money, heavy debts, coming due shortly, about which she confides in her brother Gerald. He sees her marriage to Charles Mereston as the best way out. Of course, Captain Montgomerie is also interested in arranging a marriage with Lady Frederick—as is Admiral Carlisle himself. At this point Paradine Fouldes—who is aware by now of Lady Frederick's money problems—confronts her with first an offer of money if she will refuse Charles's marriage proposal, and then, that approach failing, with the threat of telling Charles about her past love affairs. Lady Frederick counters by producing a packet of letters that reveals that Paradine's sister's late husband—instead of being the paragon of strict morality—was actually carrying on a love affair. Surprisingly, Lady Frederick then gives Paradine the opportunity of destroying them. But he refuses and they leave each other with renewed respect. It is then, though, that Lady Frederick receives her first offer of marriage: from Captain Montgomerie. And when he is rejected, he threatens her with a debt that her brother Gerald owes him.

The marriage plans of Gerald and Rose progress well, but Lady Frederick's financial difficulties worsen as she learns that the bills coming due in two days have been taken care of already by some unknown person. To make matters even worse, her dressmaker arrives insisting on payment of a past bill—but Lady Frederick skillfully reverses the situation and sends the dressmaker off ashamed and apologizing for troubling her with such an unimportant matter. Captain

Montgomerie once more presses his proposal of marriage—making clear his intention through this marriage to enter high society—and produces the negotiated bills: clear and paid for if she consents to marry him. Meanwhile, Lady Mereston attempts to persuade Charles not to marry Lady Frederick. But since Charles will hear nothing unfavorable about Lady Frederick without her being there, he sends for her to hear his mother's charges. Whereupon, Lady Mereston produces a letter that Lady Frederick wrote admitting an affair with a married man. However, Lady Frederick confesses—convincingly—that she wrote the letter only to protect the real offender, a sister-in-law, who is now dead. At this point, Lady Frederick sends for the packet of letters written by Lady Mereston's late husband to his mistress. But instead of revealing the contents—known now only to Paradine Fouldes, and the audience, of course—she burns them. Then, when she announces that she is soon leaving Monte Carlo, Charles apologizes for his mother's behavior and proposes to Lady Frederick. But she refuses to give an answer until the next day.

When Charles arrives the next morning to repeat his proposal, Lady Frederick receives him into her dressing room and completely makes up her face and does her hair in front of him—forcing him, and the audience, to see much of the artificiality of her beauty. It is somewhat a relief to Charles, then, when she refuses his proposal. Gerald and Rose arrive to announce that the Admiral has paid the debt Gerald owed to Montgomerie. It is at this point that Lady Frederick receives her next marriage proposal: this one from Admiral Carlisle himself, a proposal she declines. Her next visitor is Captain Montgomerie, who comes with bills in hand, demanding that she marry him. Fortunately, Paradine Fouldes—who has watched all of these events—intervenes: writes a check for the amount of the debt, thereby ending at once all of Montgomerie's threats and demands. It is then that Lady Frederick receives her final proposal of marriage: this one from Paradine, a proposal she happily accepts.

On opening night Maugham was in the audience. Lady Helen Mary Maugham, Maugham's brother Frederic's wife, was also present. She wrote in her diary: "Willie was pale and silent. He sat at the back of the box. The play . . . is very witty and interesting. I believe it will prove a success with the public."[2] And it did. As Walter P. Eaton reported, "The smart epigrams of this play were soon town talk, and Mr. Maugham, the neglected, found himself suddenly besieged for more plays."[3]

Maugham's targets for this comedy of manners[4] were appropriate for an Edwardian audience, critical now of the institutions of the Victorian era: religion, politics, and marriage. But one of the principal reasons that the play was such a sensation was the scene in the third act in which Lady Frederick makes herself up and puts her hair up onstage—in front of Charles. While noting Maugham's careful study of Wilde, Pinero, and Jones, Curtis states that there is no precedent in English drama for this "make up scene": it was an invention of Maugham's that for later audiences would be "amusing"—but for Edwardian audiences it was a "sensation."[5] Richard Cordell's evaluation of the play is noteworthy: "a mildly amusing example of artificial Edwardian comedy . . . snappy with witticisms and . . . agreeably nonsensical in story and character."[6]

On the whole the reception of *Lady Frederick* was favorable. The *London Times* called it "quite exhilarating entertainment."[7] But most reviewers noted its entertaining quality. The *Graphic* stated that, while *Lady Frederick* was "not a great play," it was nevertheless "thoroughly enjoyable."[8] One of the most positive reviews came from Reginald Turner, Oscar Wilde's friend, who called it a "witty, original and exquisitely-wrought study of a fascinating personality."[9]

When the play began its ninety-six-run performance in New York with Ethel Barrymore playing the lead, the *New York Sun* referred to the play as "full of brilliant snappy dialogue and well-drawn character."[10] And even the less favorable reviews admitted Maugham's capacity to entertain: the *Academy* spoke of its "charming flippancy"[11] and the *New York Dramatic Mirror* observed that it has "brilliant dialogue without much heart or much soul."[12]

For Maugham, the success of *Lady Frederick* represented the end of ten years with little to show for his efforts and the beginning of greater recognition. The preceding ten years, however, had been productive: seven novels, a volume of short stories, and a travel book. Thirty years later, Maugham wrote:

When *Lady Frederick* was produced I had reached the end of the little money I had come into when I was twenty-one, my novels did not bring me in enough to live upon, and I could earn nothing by journalism. . . . If *Lady Frederick* was a failure it seemed to me that there was nothing for me but to go back to the hospital for a year to refresh my knowledge of medicine and then get a post as a surgeon on a ship. (*SU,* 104)

Thus, although never poor, Maugham, like his character Lady Frederick, had economic worries. The success of this play, he wrote in his *Notebook,* "freed me from financial uncertainties that were never quite absent from my thoughts. I hate poverty. I hated having to scrape and save so as to make both ends meet" (*WN,* 69).

And Maugham's success was spectacular: "Three months later [after *Lady Frederick* began its run at the Court Theatre] *Mrs. Dot* was being played at the Comedy and *Jack Straw* at the Vaudeville. And in June, Lewis Walker put on *The Explorer* at the Lyric" (*SU,* 114). But even without counting the earnings that he received from the *Explorer,* by 1908 Maugham was earning "at least $1,000 a week for the three other plays."[13] Of this success Maugham wrote in his *Notebook:* "I always expected it, and when it came I accepted it as so natural that I didn't see anything to make a fuss about" (*WN,* 69).

However truthful we may consider statements by Maugham about success or the importance of money ("the sixth sense without which one can not enjoy the other five" [*SU,* 112]) to be, we must not overlook the important contribution that these plays made to the drama of England at this time. Richard Cordell observes that Maugham helped revive comedy of manners on the English stage and with Shaw, Barker, and others "affronted the stodginess and hyperorthodoxy of the backward theatre with vigorous expression of startling unconventional views. . . ."[14]

But with the success of these plays Maugham had reached his goal: "I had achieved what I wanted," he wrote years later (*SU,* 116). And he determined not to lose it, but to use the freedom that success gave him in order to make some changes in his plays: "I had no intention of fizzling out with a passing success, and I wrote the next two plays to consolidate my hold on the public. They were a little bolder and mild and unsophisticated as they must seem now, they were attacked by the most strait-laced for their indecency" (*SU,* 119). Then believing that he had now learned the techniques of drama and having had "an uninterrupted series of successes," Maugham felt it "time to try my hand at more serious work. I waited to see what I could do with more sophisticated subjects. . . . I wrote *The Tenth Man* and *Landed Gentry,* and finally after it had been lying in my desk a dozen years, produced *Loaves and Fishes.*" The result: "None of them was a failure; none of them was a success" (*SU,* 119).

Like a good journalist, a good playwright, Maugham believed, must have certain gifts: "a quick eye for a good story and a telling point, animation and a vivid way of writing" (*SU*, 122). And during these years he filled his notebook with possibilities for plays. An entry such as the following from 1908 makes it clear that Maugham was alert for a story with irony and with a definite discrepancy between appearance and reality. In this entry Maugham tells of a certain philanthropist who achieved greatness largely because of his lectures on the danger of drinking. One room in his home only he entered. Upon his sudden death and following the funeral his curious family broke into that room:

They found it full of empty bottles, bottles of brandy, whiskey, gin, bottles of chartreuse, benedictine and kummel. It was only too plain that he had brought the bottles in with him one by one and having drunk their contents had not known how to get rid of them. I would give a great deal to know what passed through his mind when he came home after delivering a temperance lecture and behind locked doors sipped green chartreuse. (*WN*, 69–70)

Burdens and Anxieties

If Maugham's goal had been simply to make a name for himself in drama and to earn a great deal of money, then he certainly would have continued in the same vein. But his particular creative and emotional makeup would not allow his life and work to be that simple. He found himself troubled by the unhappiness of his past and—more than most critics have admitted—by his present life. He speaks of these as "ghosts" that must be laid to rest. "I was but just firmly established as a playwright when I began to be obsessed by the teeming memories of my past life" (*SU*, 190). And perhaps more at this point than at any other time, his life influenced his work: "it all came back to me so pressingly, in my sleep, on my walks, when I was rehearsing plays, when I was at a party, it became such a burden to me that I made up mind that I could only regain my peace by writing it all down in the form of a novel" (*SU*, 190).

The novel, *Of Human Bondage,* his longest, most significant, and emotionally and intellectually most demanding, was written between 1911 and 1914. It represented a new direction in his career, a direction that he did not fully understand at the time. Certainly Frohman, his literary agent, did not understand: "It was impossible to combine the labour of such a project with the pressures of the theatre. . . .

Frohman was horrified at the prospect of his most money-spinning author shutting down. . . ." Of course, as Curtis observes, this decision would be "unthinkable" if Maugham's goal had been simply to make a lot of money."[15]

In 1912, however, Maugham interrupted his writing of this novel to write yet another play, *The Land of Promise*, modeled in part after Shakespeare's *The Taming of the Shrew*. According to Morgan, *The Land of Promise* was completed in 1913, and *Of Human Bondage* shortly thereafter.[16] Both works portray the incompatible relationships between men and women and end with a relationship that is more compatible than artistically convincing.

Maugham characteristically worked from live models for his characters. In this way he achieved an authenticity in his works through the use of experiences and emotions that either he had had himself or that others whom he had closely observed had had.

It is particularly revealing of Maugham's method of composing to view his life in relation to these two works. With *Of Human Bondage* Maugham's use of his past life has certainly been well documented. As Calder writes: "Literary sleuths have searched for the woman who was the basis for Mildred [a woman whom Philip, the protagonist, loves hopelessly and helplessly], but there have so far been no startling revelations"; "although it is almost certain that Maugham underwent some of the unfortunate experiences which provided the basis for Philip's suffering, Mildred is probably largely a fictional creation."[17] But so far little consideration has been given to the experiences that Maugham was having in the present, at the time of the composition of these two works. In 1911, at the beginning of the composition, for instance, Maugham first met Syrie Wellcome, an unhappily married woman who was being unfaithful to her husband ("the most prominent of her lovers then was Gordan Selfridge")[18] and whom Maugham would eventually marry. They would have a daughter, and later divorce. At this time Maugham was still seeing Sue Jones although he was becoming increasingly irritated by her promiscuity, "sharing her with his friends."[19] It was at this point that Maugham decided to put an end to his eight-year love affair with Sue Jones by marrying her. More than twenty years later Maugham reflected upon his reason for this decision and the decisions to follow:

I was forty. If I meant to marry and have children it was high time I did so, and for some time I had amused my imagination with pictures of myself in the married state. There was no one I particularly wanted to marry [but

in fact there was in 1913: Sue Jones]. It was the condition that attracted me
[the truth here in this statement is no doubt in Morgan's observations about
marriage as a cover for Maugham's homosexuality—which would eventually
become his sexual preference for the rest of his life]. It seemed a necessary
motif in the pattern of life that I had designed, and to my ingenuous fancy
(for though no longer young and thinking myself worldly wise, I was still
in many ways incredibly naive) it offered peace; peace from the disturbance
of love affairs, casual it might be in the beginning, but bringing in their
train such troublesome complications (for it takes two to make a love affair
and a man's meat is too often a woman's poison); peace that would enable
me to write all I wanted to write without the loss of precious time or disturbance of mind; peace and a settled and dignified way of life. (*SU,* 193)

Seen in light of the events of his life at this time, these incredible
statements clarify as well as disguise much of the motivation for
Maugham's actions. Before noting Maugham's statements that follow
these, it would be well to examine such events. In 1913—having
completed *The Land of Promise*—Maugham traveled to Chicago (he
had made his first trip to the United States three years earlier) and
proposed marriage to Sue Jones. She rejected his offer—willing to
continue the affair, but not to marry him (*L,* 111).

Perhaps this long bondage to Sue Jones—despite her affairs with
other men, including several of his friends—and the bitterness and
frustration of rejection were the basis for Philip's bondage to Mildred.
Despite her unfaithfulness, lack of devotion, and fondness for his
friends, Philip could not free himself from this bondage. But undoubtedly there were earlier and later bondages in Maugham's long
life.

The Wish For Dignity

On the rebound, Maugham turned to Syrie and eventually began
what he hoped—although not with the intensity and excitement of
the former relationship—would be comfortable and he would be in a
pleasant, undisturbed way "happy." No doubt these experiences are
the basis for the anticipated peaceful life for Frank and Norah at the
end of *The Land of Promise* and the anticipated comfortable marriage
and uneventful life ahead for Philip and Sally at the end of *Of Human
Bondage.*

In statements that follow those quoted above, Maugham analyzes
his motivation and the relationship between his life and his writing

at this time in his career: "I sought freedom and thought I could find it in marriage. I conceived these notions when I was still at work on *Of Human Bondage*, and turning my wishes into fiction, as writers will, toward the end of it I drew a picture of the marriage I should have liked to make" (*SU*, 193–94). In short, these works end with the "dignified way of life" that Maugham wished for.

In *The Land of Promise*, evidently completed before his rejection by Sue Jones (Morgan reports: "Rejected Maugham returns to London to bury himself in rehearsals of *The Land of Promise*"), Maugham clearly portrays the influence of his present experiences: his desire for happiness and peace, his concern for economic security, his interest and respect for the unconventional, adventuresome ways of the non-English people and environments. Norah, a lady's companion to Miss Wynne, expects upon her employer's death to receive an inheritance. Unfortunately, when the will is read, it is discovered that Miss Wynne never changed the will—as she promised Norah she would. As a result, Norah must move to Canada and live with her brother and his wife. However, Norah and her brother's wife simply cannot live under the same roof, and in a rash decision Norah accepts Frank Taylor's offer of a business-contract-type marriage. The following dialogue takes place shortly before this rash act.

NORAH [*to Taylor*]: You wouldn't talk about it [marrying] like that unless you looked down upon women. Oh, I pity the poor wretched creature who becomes your wife.

TAYLOR: I guess she won't have a bad time when I've broken her into my ways.

NORAH: Are you under the impression you can do that?

TAYLOR: Yep.

NORAH: You're not expecting that there'll be much love lost between you and the girl you—honour with your choice?

TAYLOR: What's love got to do with it? It's a business proposition. (*CP*, 2:247)

Norah has an accurate estimate of Taylor (and Maugham of human nature), for earlier she had remarked about him to her brother: "He shouldn't joke. He's got no sense of humour." Theirs is a marriage, then, founded not upon love but upon mutual need: he for a companion and coworker, she for financial support and escape from her sister-in-law. As in Maugham's earlier works, the characters here are sensitive to social class. In fact, this marriage is similar to that between Bertha and Craddock in *Mrs. Craddock:* a refined woman married to a rough, uneducated hired man. And, as in later works such as the short story "The Outstation," British characters will measure their present life by their past life in England and even by what is going on in the present in England. Thus Norah's remark: "I wonder what they're doing in England now. . . . When I think of England I always think of it at teatime" (*CP*, 2:272). Of course, these statements anticipate further comparisons and contrasts.

Founded on a story he had heard from an aunt whose companion went to live with a brother in Canada and who eventually married a hired man, this play was one that needed grounding in Maugham's own experience. Accordingly, he traveled to Canada to experience the hardship of the wilderness firsthand. Describing the oppressive winter conditions—an atmosphere comparable to Stanley Kubrick's production of *The Shining*—Maugham wrote to a friend:

My God, what a life they lead, at least in the winter, surrounded by the snowy prairie, cut off from their neighbors and absorbed with the struggle of getting three meals a day. Husbands and wives get to such a pitch of irritability that they will pass weeks without speaking to one another. In one house in which I stayed the wife had killed herself, in another there hung a strange gloom of impending madness. I was glad to get away.[20]

In the play, of course, Maugham creates characters who are participants in this environment—such as Norah: "Month after month I used to sit looking at the prairie and sometimes I wanted to scream at the top of my voice just to break the silence. I thought I should never escape. The shack was like a prison. I was hemmed in by the snow and the cold and the stillness" (*CP*, 2:304).

After their marriage, conflict between Frank and Norah is inevitable. As the *New York Times* drama critic wrote after opening night on Christmas 1919, "Norah [was] rebellious and Frank determined to be master in his own house."[21] Refusing to wash the dishes on the table, Norah boxes Frank's ears when he attempts to make her do so. They argue, Norah kicks and bites Frank, and she throws the dishes onto the floor and breaks them. After an attempt to force her to sweep up the broken cups, Taylor says:

Look here, if you don't clean up that mess at once, I'll give you the biggest hiding you've ever had in your life. . . [*He turns up the sleeves of his sweater. Suddenly she bursts into loud cries.*]

NORAH: Help! Help! Help!

TAYLOR: What's the good of that? There ain't no one within a mile of us. Listen. [*He puts up his finger and seems to listen intently. She looks at him, but does not speak.*] . . . Listen to the silence. Can't you hear it, the silence of the prairie? Why, we might be the only two people in the world, you and me, here in this shack right out in the prairie. Listen. There ain't a sound. It might be the garden of Eden. What's that about male and female created He them? I guess you're my wife, my girl, and I want you. (*CP,* 2:278–80, 286)

The *London Sunday Times* reviewer, J. T. Gerin (1 March 1914) was impressed with the power of this scene: "It was a sad wedding night. No romance, but all work—menial work exacted by a commanding voice. She remained the lady and defied the man. She gave tit-for-tat. . . . there was no way—to accept the yoke of matrimony with all it implied. She passed to the adjoining chamber as one going to doom."

When spring comes, though, Norah has brightened up the shack and expects a visit shortly from her brother Ed. When he does arrive he brings Reggie Hornby, a fellow countryman who, after spending a year in Canada (at his father's insistence because of large gambling debts Reggie has acquired), now looks forward to returning to England. Reggie, like Blake's Thel, retreats to the security of the homeland. But Norah has developed a new view of England and of life, a view that she does not yet fully understand: "I suppose it's being alone with the prairie all these months, things which used to seem rather funny and clever, well, I see them quite differently now" (*CP,* 2:295).

And with him on this visit Ed has brought two letters: one from Miss Pringle in England offering her a position and another from the solicitor enclosing a check for five hundred pounds from the family of her late employer. Mrs. Sharp, a neighbor, arrives at this point to tell Norah of crop failure threatened by a weed that may shortly be the ruin of both of their farms. Norah does her best to console Mrs. Sharp. Shortly thereafter the neighbor returns to say that their crop is safe, at least most of it. Alone, Norah and Frank talk about the future, Norah deciding to return to England, Frank agreeing to allow her to go. It is then, though, that Norah realizes that she has grown in love with Frank. And she recalls the way she praised life in Canada to cheer up Mrs. Sharp—that life here has more of what is vital and real than one could ever hope to find in England: "It's bitter work opening up a new country and perhaps it's others who reap the harvest. But I wonder if those who start don't get a reward that the later comers never dream of" (*CP,* 2:301). Understandably, then, when Frank breaks the news to her that their crop is ruined and he will have to go to work for another farmer, Norah hands him the check for five hundred pounds.

In many ways *The Land of Promise* is a play unlike Maugham's earlier plays—such as the comedy of manners *Lady Frederick,* discussed above. Although it ends happily, the play is serious in tone. Aware of this same seriousness about the work, the drama critic of the *Academy* wrote about the 1914 London performance that Maugham sought to deal with "hidden intimacies of life."[22]

Chapter Five
Autobiographical Novel

It is of critical importance to understand the significance of *Of Human Bondage* in Maugham's writing career. The psychological dynamics of Maugham's writing this novel are closer to that experienced by writers of autobiography than that experienced by most autobiographical novelists. Maugham wrote this novel later in life, after having established himself in a variety of types of writing: novel, short story, drama, travel book (in contrast to Joyce's *Portrait of the Artist as a Young Man* and Lawrence's *Sons and Lovers*, which were early works). Second, since this work came later in his career, he was able to draw from his writing experience and to make use of a variety of writing skills—chiefly dramatic—that he had acquired (comparable to those of St. Augustine, Mill, Newman—giving order to their past life). And when *Of Human Bondage* was written, Maugham was living the middle period of his life, a period in which many experience what psychologists call "a mid-life crisis." It is in this period that autobiographers look back over their life to find a pattern, justification, meaning. The more literary and gifted autobiographers typically go beyond their own lives to become more universal and philosophical. Such was the case in *Of Human Bondage*.

Reshaping Life

But above all, the importance of this novel is that in writing it Maugham moved a step further toward understanding his strength as a writer, toward developing his own aesthetic. Curtis refers to Maugham's "need to reshape life into a pattern" and calls it his "greatest drive."[1] This need and drive took form in this novel, his greatest accomplishment in shaping life into art. In the theater he had developed his "reshaping," dramatic skills far beyond those displayed in the 1898 "The Artistic Temperament of Stephen Carey". He became more fully aware of his best subject matter—experience. With the distance and maturity now of almost thirty years, he turned his acute powers of observation and analysis on himself. And in the novel, he wisely decided upon an external, third-person omniscient narrator. Maugham wrote of this shaping of experience—direct or observed—as creating "a plausible harmony": "People are too elusive, too shadowy, to be copied; and they are also too incoherent and contradictory. The writer does not copy his originals; he takes what he wants from them, a few traits that have caught his attention, a turn of mind that has fired his imagination and thereupon constructs his characters" (*SU*, 209–10).

Understandably, Ward notes: "Maugham's best stories are too well-formed to be personal experiences transferred direct to paper."[2] The important point here, though, is that Maugham is at his best when his characters, events, emotions, and attitudes are grounded in personal experience. He is at his weakest when he goes beyond his experience. In 1911, in composing *Of Human Bondage,* Maugham was digging back into the personal experience of "The Artistic Temperament of Stephen Carey." As Curtis observes, he "needed now to go more deeply into the causes of his peculiar sense of alienation from life in the midst of so much prosperity, to follow his own emotional and intellectual progress throughout those early years with great but not absolute fidelity to fact."[3]

Somerset Maugham's motivation for writing and his use of personal experience in his writing are therefore not simple matters. But there is considerable evidence that Maugham depended upon experience and upon models for characters from individuals he had either known personally or observed. And because the experiences during the composition of *The Land of Promise* and *Of Human Bondage* were especially traumatic, they had a far reaching influence upon his life. It is little wonder, then, the emotions and dilemmas that he was presently experiencing would be for Maugham a rich source of inspiration. As Naik observes, in his early works Maugham developed two important faculties: "the deep sensibility which was, very soon, to create among the best of Maugham's novels, *Of Human Bondage,* and the flair for satirical observation which was to develop into the cold indifference and cynicism of his later works."[4]

Returning to the composition of *Of Human Bondage* after having his marriage proposal rejected by Sue Jones, after completing *The Land of Promise,* and after beginning a relationship with Syrie Wellcome, Maugham drew upon his major strengths—strengths that he would eventually come to know as well as he then knew his limitations: (1) the transformation of experience and observations into fiction and (2) the dramatic skills developed in the theater. The first strength, use of personal experience and observations, should be evident in a large degree from the above discussion. How much Maugham had developed the second strength, his dramatic skill, can be seen by contrasting *Of Human Bondage* with "The Artistic Temperament of Stephen Carey."

Of Human Bondage opens with the death of Philip's mother. Orphaned, Philip is forced to move from his French home to England. There he lives with his Uncle Carey, vicar of Blackstable, and Aunt Louisa. They are childless and live a life quite unsuitable for their nine-year-old nephew, who speaks French more fluently than English and has a clubfoot. Shortly, Philip is sent to school at Tercanberry where he is mistreated by students and masters for his physical handicap. One holiday back at the vicarage he has an unusual experience. Having read in the Bible that if a person has faith enough mountains can be moved, he decides to put his faith to the test by praying, believing with all his might, that his handicap will be removed. When this fails, his disappointment is the first step toward his eventual loss of faith. Ill and with a determination not to abide the bullying of his masters, Philip spends a year studying in Heidelberg. It is there that he loses even more confidence in his childhood faith in God. Under the influence of two fellow lodgers, one an American and the other an Englishman, Philip comes to what for him is an exhilarating and freeing conclusion that there is no God. Upon his return to England Philip meets Miss Wilkinson, a relative of one of his aunt's close German friends. It is with her that he has his first sexual experience.

A brief trial with the accounting business as a possible career proves disappointing. He next journeys to Paris to study art for two years. But at the end of that time, realizing he will never be more than average, Philip gives it all up.

Finally, against his uncle's best thinking, Philip enters St. Thomas's Hospital in London in order to study for a career in medicine. And it is during these early years of his training that he meets Mildred Rogers, a waitress at the A.B.C. shop, a meeting that will lead to a bondage of passion. Philip will be unable to free himself from this bondage for some time. As his passion for Mildred grows, he makes repeated advances: invitations, suggestions, usually meeting with rejections, or more characteristically indifference—Mildred's typical reply is: "I don't mind." When one day she goes away with another, Miller by name, Philip feels that he has finally lost her forever. He does not pass his examinations. At this time he finds a friend in No-rah Nesbitt, an individual who has a greater interest in him than he in her—the reverse of his earlier relationship with Mildred. Their friendship, though, is genuine and they are good for each other. Philip makes progress toward his examinations. But later Mildred returns, this time expecting a child. He helps, of course, providing her and her child with a home, but without the earlier physical love for her. In fact, it is when he refuses to yield to her seductive advances that Mildred flies into a rage, and disappears completely. Philip again adjusts. He returns to Norah, but it is too late: she has found another and plans to be married soon. It is then that Mildred again returns: her child has died, and she is now a common streetwalker, and she is in ill health. As before, Philip takes her in. While Mildred has been away Philip has made several changes: because of his money problems, he is now working in a department store; he has made friends with a Mr. Athelny, a fellow employee, and his family; and he has begun once more to prepare for his medical examinations.

Mildred leaves Philip's life for good when she angrily reacts to Philip's insistence that she quit prostitution because of its danger to her health. Philip experiences another loss in the death of Cronshaw, his old friend from Paris. And while in the British Museum, Philip recalls Cronshaw's statement that the meaning of life could be found in a Persian rug, and concludes that life had no pattern, no meaning. If an individual is to find meaning, he reasons, then that pattern must be put into life by the individual. The friendship and concern of the Athelnys become increasingly important at this time in Philip's life. Their oldest daughter, Sally, Philip finds attractive. The interest is mutual and they soon become quite fond of each other. When they have sex, they both worry for fear of a pregnancy. When Philip discovers that their fears are unfounded, he finds to his surprise that he still wants to marry Sally, even though he does not love her: to bring a pattern, a meaning to a life that he has discovered has no integral meaning.

Dramatic Skill

Contrasting the opening chapters of "The Artistic Temperament of Stephen Carey" (1898)—dealing with the loss of Stephen's mother and his humiliation at school—with comparable opening chapters in *Of Human Bondage* (1915) will make clear how much Maugham had strengthened his dramatic capabilities. Chapter 1 of "The Artistic

Temperament of Stephen Carey" opens with Stephen playing with a theater, a present for his ninth birthday.[5] Although there is no dialogue, the external omniscient narrator lets us know that Stephen has seen *Hamlet* (did not like it because of the inartistic ending—killing so many people off) and that he likes *Waterloo*. In fact, he has a great battle with his soldiers in the theater and when *Waterloo* is finished only the Duke of Wellington (a national hero throughout the Victorian era) lives. His masterpiece, though, is "The Corsica Brothers with Louis of France." The hero cries at the end that he is avenged and the curtain falls. And Stephen, alone throughout this entire opening chapter, is completely thrilled. The scene has no dialogue.

Then, in the second chapter, pages 8–16, Misses Fordlington and Emma have been talking in another room and come into the one where Stephen is playing. Putting him on her lap, Emma rocks and consoles him. He decides, as in *Of Human Bondage,* to go in to see the others so they will feel sorry for him. And they do. But in talking about his father, Dr. Carey, and his mother, Sophia, they soon forget about Stephen. He may well, though, have understood the drift of these remarks—similar to those in *Of Human Bondage*—that there is little money left for his education, his mother was a woman of society—quite unconcerned about money, and her death was in some ways a blessing.

Finally, in chapter 3, pages 17–23, Stephen is on the way back to the house with Emma and he asks her to tell him a story. She tells him a story of a boy who would not wash his hands or comb his hair. But Emma is mostly worried about the position she will lose and the economic consequences associated with its loss. And Stephen wonders about his Uncle John, who will arrive in four days. When they reach the house Stephen becomes aware for the first time that he is now an orphan. He has an emotional moment in his mother's bedroom—similar to that in *Of Human Bondage*—in which he senses his mother's presence but realizes that she will never be there again. And he cries genuine tears.

In contrast, in the opening three chapters of *Of Human Bondage*[6] Maugham devotes more attention to what the characters say. The first chapter in *Of Human Bondage,* for instance, opens with a brief paragraph describing the setting—the weather: "gray," "dull," "clouds," "rawness in the air," "snow"; a woman servant coming into the room where a child, Philip, is sleeping; a stucco house next door, and a child's bed. Then the sound of voices: "Wake up, Philip"—

pulling down bed clothes, taking the child in her arms, carrying the child (now half awake) downstairs—"Your mother wants you." And, although at this point only eighty-seven words into a very long novel, Maugham has skillfully prepared his audience for the dramatic scene of Philip's being with his dying mother for the last time. The entire scene is presented with the detachment of a dramatist: we learn of the nature of the circumstances mainly through dialogue.

> [PHILIP'S MOTHER:]   Oh, don't take him away yet.
>
> [THE DOCTOR:]   What's the matter? . . . You're tired . . . [*To the nurse:*] You'd better put him back in his bed.
>
> [PHILIP'S MOTHER:]   What will happen to him, poor child? . . .
>
> [THE DOCTOR:]   What about the little boy? I should think he'd be better out of the way.
>
> [THE NURSE:]   Miss Watkin said she'd take him, sir.
>
> [THE DOCTOR:]   Who's she?
>
> [THE NURSE:]   She's his godmother, sir. D'you think Mrs. Carey will get over it, sir? (*OHB*, 1–3)

The external, omniscient, narrator ends chapter 1 with a succinct description of the doctor's response, an early example of Maugham's use of nonverbal behavior for dramatic effect: "The doctor shook his head" (*OHB*, 3).

In chapter 2 Maugham follows the same pattern: setting the scene—"a week later," "Philip . . . an only child . . . used to amusing himself"; "hides himself from the Red Indian . . . ," "hearing the door open"; and then dialogue. The external narrator provides what any dramatist could provide visually on stage: "It was in eighteen-eighty-five and she wore a bustle. Her gown was of black velvet, with tight sleeves and sloping shoulders, and the skirt had three large flounces. She wore a black bonnet with velvet strings. She hesitated. The questions she had expected did not come, and so she could not give the answer she had prepared" (*OHB*, 3). The black dress, in keeping with the nature of the occasion, increases the dramatic irony of the following scene.

> [EMMA:]   Aren't you going to ask how your mamma is? . . .
>
> [PHILIP:]   Oh, I forgot. How is mamma? . . .
>
> [EMMA:]   Your mamma is quite well and happy.

[PHILIP:]   Oh, I'm glad.

[EMMA:]   Your mamma's gone away. You won't ever see her any more. . . .

[PHILIP:]   Why not?

[EMMA:]   Your mamma's in heaven. (*OHB,* 3–4)

The narrator describes Emma's genuineness, which contrasts with the self-seeking nurse's falseness in Maugham's earlier work: "Her tears increased her emotion, and she pressed the little boy to her heart. She felt vaguely the pity of that child deprived of the only love in the world that is quite unselfish. It seemed dreadful that he must be handed over to strangers" (*OHB,* 4). And Philip, though not fully understanding, cried with her.

What follows is the scene—described fully in chapter 2—in which Philip says goodbye to Miss Watkin, knowing full well, of course, that she will feel sorry for him. And she does. Then, announcing that he must go home, Philip limps out of the room:

[MISS WATKIN:]   His mother was my greatest friend. I can't bear to think that she's dead.

[OTHERS PRESENT:]   Poor little boy, it's dreadful to think of him quite alone in the world. I see he limps.

Yes, he's got a club-foot. It was such a grief to his mother. (*OHB,* 5)

Thus, in two chapters (covering less than five pages) Maugham has presented two dramatic scenes—with the objectivity of a dramatist who is restricted to the conversations and actions of the characters of a play. And Maugham has made the important alteration from the earlier version, transforming Stephen's stammer into Philip's club-foot, a handicap that would have a greater dramatic impact upon the audience.

Chapter 3 (slightly over five pages in length) finds Philip returning to his home, meeting his uncle, and—as in the earlier version—visiting his mother's room for the last time: "Philip opened a large cupboard filled with dresses and stepping in, took as many of them as he could in his arms and buried his face in them. They smelt of the scent his mother used. Then he pulled open the drawers, filled with his mother's things, and looked at them. . . ." Here Maugham captures the psychological situation of a bereaved child, still in shock, unable to accept the reality of his mother's death—especially in a culture that speaks of death and dying euphemistically ("gone to heaven"): "It was not true that he would never see her again. It was not true simply because it was impossible. He climbed up on the bed and put his head on the pillow. He lay there quite still" (*OHB*, 9).

The importance of this dramatic presentation to Maugham's development as a writer—with the objective, external narrator and with the unfolding of Philip's character through dialogue—can not be overemphasized. One of Maugham's earliest critics, Ward, noted Maugham's method of involving the reader in the drama of Philip's quest for meaning: "One has never heard of Philip Carey spoken of by readers with anything but compassion, and that compassion must have been realized in them as they read. The secret is that Philip . . . does not indulge in self-pity. . . . He accepts, and acceptance of one's own suffering must bring tolerance toward it. . . ."[7] Considering the novel to be "Maugham's most complete statement of the importance of physical and spiritual liberty," Calder expresses an admiration similar to Ward's: "His achievement is a novel which finds its power in absolute sincerity and honesty. Maugham has managed consummately to use an artificial framework, yet convey real life."[8] Of course, the objectivity of the Maugham persona is not new. Of this persona Calder observes: "the aloof character of the Maugham *persona* owes its origin to this professional characteristic . . . the discipline inherent in his studies helped him to avoid the moralizing or sentimentalizing. . . . the objectivity which a doctor develops in order to treat his patients without causing an unbearable emotional strain on himself was combined with Maugham's natural reticence to give him a detachment which he retained throughout his career."[9]

Whether one regards Maugham's medical training as the major factor behind the clinical, objective narrative style or simply Maugham's basic temperament and approach to life, the result is the same. In contrast to eighteenth- and nineteenth-century narratives—in which the narrator (of, for instance, *Tom Jones, Waverley, David Copperfield*) not only provides descriptions but also interpretations of each event, motives of characters, etc.—*Of Human Bondage* presents events and characters largely without interpretation by the narrator. In fact, the reader is not urged to adopt any definite conclusions; events and characters are rarely interpreted. Rather, like the Persian rug, what meaning the reader ultimately finds in the novel he or she must put into it. The existential crisis that Philip inevitably faces is also faced by the reader. And whether or not the reader's conclusions are the same as Philip's, he or she must nevertheless struggle toward meaning—as Philip struggles. In fact, Philip is not an altogether admirable character: self-centered, overly sensitive, frequently depressed, generally pessimistic, often tending toward masochism. Nevertheless, as readers, we never forget the dramatic scene opening the novel. And Philip's sensitivity is psychologically sound: handicapped children orphaned early in life often interpret life as Philip does. As Richard Cordell has observed, we all have experiences similar to those of Philip: Maugham "leads a reader to ask himself questions about good and evil, reward and punishment, justice and injustice, fact and superstition, the good life and the wasted life."[10]

Use of Dialogue

Maugham exploits his skill with dialogue in this novel. All but three of the one hundred twenty-two chapters follow the same pattern as the first three discussed above: succinct description, explanation, background as preparation for the sound of voices; then conversation, voices, dialogue. Maugham had served out his apprenticeship in the theater so well that each chapter reads as if it were a scene in a play. And the scenes consequently have an authenticity about them that rings through the very tone and dialectal style of the characters. The reader hears what the characters speak, rather than being told what they say—thereby coming to know them more fully and their relationship to each other.

Even in these three chapter/scenes (6, 7, 31) in which there are no sounds of a voice or voices, the narrator provides important background information and thereby prepares the reader for subsequent conversation. In chapter 6, for example, the narrator explains how one day at the vicarage is very much like another. He includes a description of bringing the *Times* to the vicar in the morning and the careful system of passing it afterward from one individual to another in the household—according to rank, of course (a device that Maugham later will use effectively in a short story entitled "The Outstation").[11] Important information is also included about key individuals in the parish. And, as he had done already in *Mrs. Craddock* and would do again in *Our Betters* and *Cakes and Ale,* Maugham captures the distinctiveness of the Kentish setting with a particularity and genuineness that he does not achieve with such settings as Paris, London, Chicago, Tahiti, Borneo—settings that are rendered more abstractly. (Of course, since Kent was his boyhood English home, this is another instance of Maugham's need to ground his fiction in his own experience.) For example, after finishing her business at the bank, Mrs. Carey—accompanied by Philip—would typically go upstairs to see the sister of the banker, Mr. Wilson, the richest man in town. And while they visited, Philip would sit in the dark, stuffy parlor watching goldfish swim in a bowl. A further example is the section in which the narrator describes the regularity of the serving of dinner at the vicarage and the usual Sunday afternoon activities. Dinner was at one o'clock and consisted of beef or mutton, except on Sunday, when they ate one of their own chickens. In the afternoons Philip did his Latin, mathematics, and French lessons, and was taught piano. Rarely did they ever have guests for tea. But when they did the guests were always Josiah Graves, the curate, and his sister, and Dr. Wigram and his wife. And when they played games, Mrs. Carey was careful to allow her husband to win because he hated losing.

Finally, the narrator completes his portrait of daily life at the vicarage with a description of the system for taking baths, a system that had to be altered when young Philip arrived. Naturally the vicar insisted that "Philip should be clean and sweet for the Lord's Day." After eighteen years of service in the house, Mary Ann protested that she would rather quit than be put out by having to bathe him. And Philip naturally insisted on bathing himself. But because she couldn't "abide a boy who wasn't properly washed," Mary Ann agreed. The narrator's description is a close approximation of Mary Ann's remarks of protest: "she'd work herself to the bone even if it was Saturday night" (OHB, 22).

In chapter 7, another chapter without the literal sound of a voice, the narrator provides the reader with a portrait of Sunday, the most important day of the week in Philip's strange new English home, "a day crowded with incident"—from getting up "half an hour earlier than usual" to going to bed after a full day. Despite the absence of dialogue at the very beginning of the chapter, the narrator gives the reader a description of the sound of a voice, a description that captures the flavor and atmosphere of the vicar's home: "No lying abed for a poor parson on the day of rest, Mr. Carey remarked as Mary Ann knocked at the door punctually at eight." On Sunday Mrs. Carey takes longer to dress, prayers are more extensive, and breakfast more substantial. Afterward Mr. Carey prepares the bread for communion and Philip is allowed to help.

The narrator provides a close substitute for dialogue in describing the verbal exchange between the characters. For instance, the narrator describes Mr. Carey's reactions: "It was extraordinary that after thirty years of marriage his wife could not be ready on Sunday morning"; "They knew that he must have an egg for his voice, there were two women in the house, and no one had the least regard for his comfort" (*OHB*, 23). The result, of course, is that Maugham achieves the breadth and range of a purely descriptive chapter, but also he accomplishes much of the depth and authenticity of a scene with dialogue.

During the sermon, Philip became "bored" and "if he fidgeted Mrs. Carey put a gentle hand on his arm and looked at him reproachfully." And, typical for a boy of his age, he "regained interest when the final hymn was sung" (*OHB*, 23). In the afternoon, after a "substantial dinner," Mrs. Carey would rest in her room and Mr. Carey would lie down on the drawing room sofa "for forty winks." At five o'clock tea Mr. Carey would eat an egg "to support himself for evensong": "Mr. Carey walked to church in the evening, and Philip limped along by his side. The walk through the darkness along the country road strangely impressed him, and the church with all its lights in the distance, coming gradually nearer, seemed very friendly" (*OHB*, 24). When they return, supper is ready and Mr. Carey's slippers are waiting for him in front of the fire, "by their side Philip's, one the shoe of a small boy, the other mishapen and odd" (*OHB*, 24). The scene comes to an end with Philip, "dreadfully tired," going up to bed: "he did not resist when Mary Ann undressed him. She kissed him after she tucked him up, and he began to love her" (*OHB*, 24–25).

In the third chapter in which the reader does not hear the sound of voices, chapter 31, it is Christmas Eve in Germany; Hayward, Philip's aesthete friend, has just left Heidelberg for Italy. The narrator gives the reader an account of Philip's ambivalent attitude toward Hayward: "Though much under Hayward's influences . . . he resented the shadow of a sneer with which Hayward looked upon his straight ways" (*OHB*, 137). In this chapter also we have a close approximation to the sound of a voice: "They corresponded. Hayward was an admirable letter-writer, and knowing his talent took pains with his letters. . . . He proposed that Philip join him in Italy: 'He

[Philip] was wasting his time at Heidelberg. The Germans were gross and life there was common; how could the soul come to her own in that . . . landscape?' " (*OHB*, 137). Again the narrator gives the reader a close approximation to the pointed, reprimanding question that Hayward could very well have put to Philip. The narrator provides the reader with certain information: that Hayward's letter made Philip restless, that Philip received an introduction to philosophy under Kuno Fischer at the University of Heidelberg, and that preparations were under way for Philip to return to England. The narrator further tells of a letter in which his aunt informs Philip that Miss Wilkinson, Mrs. Carey's friend who made the arrangements for Philip's year in Heidelberg, would be at the vicarage when he returned and would spend a few weeks there. Finally, the narrator tells the reader that Philip "had been thinking of nothing but the future; and he went without regret" (*OHB*, 139). Maugham's use of dialogue, of the sound or approximate sound of the voice is a major strength of this novel. It gives authenticity and concreteness to the characters and settings.

Preparation for Bondage

Furthermore, throughout the novel Maugham carefully prepares the reader for Philip's bondage of passion, principally through Philip's relationship with Miss Wilkinson and Fanny Price and the bondage of passion that these individuals have to Philip. These relationships foreshadow Philip's subsequent bondage to Mildred.

Returning home from Heidelberg Philip is greeted by a genuinely joyous Aunt Louisa and Miss Wilkinson, a governess by profession, whom he had never met before. He and she quickly become friends and spend much of the day together: talking, and walking; and she gives him voice lessons. Although she is much older, their relationship soon becomes quite flirtatious. One day she tells him a story about an art student living above her apartment who kept writing her passionate love letters. Finally, she received one of his letters saying he was coming that very evening to make passionate love to her. As she read the letter in her apartment she imagined how he would ring the door bell and how she would refuse to answer. Just then, she looked up. He was standing there in front of her. She had forgotten to shut the door.

The story affects Philip strangely. He soon begins to work up his courage to kiss her. He determines to make full conquest of Miss Wilkinson and persuades her, without much difficulty, to receive him in her bedroom one night. Driven more by sheer determination than desire, Philip meets her in her room and they make love. For Miss Wilkinson ("Emily," as she insists upon Philip calling her), it is a genuine love she feels for him. And Philip shows himself an "eager" but detached lover. "He was deliciously flattered to discover that Miss Wilkinson was in love with him. . . . When he kissed her it was wonderful to feel the passion that seemed to thrill her soul." From their first meeting he determined that "he ought to make love to her. . . ." (*OHB*, 152).

Yet Philip is ambivalent; the thought of Miss Wilkinson and the anticipation of making love to her are much more exciting than Miss Wilkinson herself or the act of making love: "When he thought of it at night in bed, or when he sat by himself in the garden reading a book, he was thrilled by it; but when he saw Miss Wilkinson it seemed less picturesque" (*OHB*, 152). "He could not imagine himself burying his face in Miss Wilkinson's hair, it always struck him as a little sticky" (*OHB*, 153). Nevertheless, he thinks it "would be very satisfactory to have an intrigue, and he thrilled with the legitimate pride he would enjoy in his conquest. He owed it to himself to seduce her" (*OHB*, 153). Even on the night of this seduction, his conquest is accompanied by a large dose of disgust at his less than ideal lover:

She had taken off her skirt and blouse, and was standing in her petticoat. It was short and only came down to the top of her boots; the upper part of it was black, of some shiny material, and there was a red flounce. She wore a camisole of white calico with short arms. She looked grotesque. Philip's heart sank as he stared at her; she had never seemed so unattractive; but it was too late now. (*OHB*, 161)

Sensing this incompatibility early in their relationship—her caring more for him and being bound by passion to him while he remains more detached and aloof—she talks with Philip about the month of leisure that they have ahead of them and their future after that. "And then you go to freedom and I to bondage," she remarks.

Another relationship that Maugham uses to prepare the reader for Philip's bondage to Mildred is that of Fanny Price to Philip. After a brief and unfortunate try in London at the accounting profession, Philip proposes trying his hand at art in Paris. At first his aunt and

uncle are shocked. Mr. Carey is dead set against it, but Mrs. Carey
has sympathy for Philip and even persuades Philip to use her own
savings to help finance his study in Paris. And it is there, in an art
class, that Philip becomes acquainted with Fanny, a hard working
but untalented student of art.

She was a girl of twenty-six with a great deal of dull gold hair; it was hand-
some hair, but it was carelessly done, dragged back from her forehead and
tied in a hurried knot. She had a large face, with broad, flat features and
small eyes; her skin was pasty, with a singular unhealthiness of tone,
and there was no colour in the cheeks. She had an unwashed air and you
could not help wondering if she slept in her clothes. (*OHB*, 195)

Mrs. Otter, who is in charge of the studio where he will study, has
placed Philip next to Fanny. "She's a disagreeable, ill-natured girl,
and she can't draw herself at all, but she knows the ropes, and she
can be useful to a newcomer if she cares to take the trouble." But
Clutton, one of the most talented of the painters, warns Philip:
"You've made an impression on Fanny Price. You'd better look out"
(*OHB*, 197).

Philip's friendliness is mistaken by Fanny as affection, and as he
fails to meet her expectations, she becomes first jealous of everyone
else, then angry, and finally depressed. She wants him to see her
drawings. But when he does, the narrator tells the reader:

He was panic-stricken. He did not know what to say. It was not only that
they were ill-drawn, or that the colour was put on amateurishly by someone
who had no eye for it; but there was no attempt at getting the values, and
the perspective was grotesque. It looked like the work of a child of five, but
a child would have had some naïveté and might at least have made an attempt to put down what he saw; but here was the work of a vulgar mind
chock full of recollections of vulgar pictures. (*OHB*, 239)

Somehow, though, he is able to lie and tell her that he likes them.
But when Philip decides to spend the summer in Moret with Lawson
and Ruth Chalice, Fanny flies into a rage:

"How filthy! I thought you were a decent fellow. You were about the
only one here. She's been with Clutton and Potter and Flanagan, even with
old Foinet—that's why he takes so much trouble about her—and now two
of you, you and Lawson. It makes me sick."

"Oh, what nonsense! She's a very decent sort. One treats her just as if she were a man."

"Oh, don't speak to me, don't speak to me."

"But what can it matter to you? . . . It's really no business of yours where I spend my summer.

I was looking forward to it so much. . . . I didn't think you had the money to go away, and there wouldn't have been anyone else here, and we could have worked together, and we'd have gone to see things." (*OHB*, 245).

Fanny's reaction—given her situation, passion for Philip, state of mind—is psychologically sound, as is her next impulse: to hurt him in every way she can:

"and I can tell you this—you can work here for a thousand years and you'll never do any good. You haven't got any talent. You haven't got any originality. And it's not only me—they all say it. You'll never be a painter as long as you live."

"That is no business of yours either, is it?"

"Oh, you think it's only my temper. Ask Clutton, ask Lawson, ask Chalice. Never, never, never. You haven't got it in you." (*OHB*, 246)

It is important here to note not only the intensity of Fanny's passion but also the extent to which Maugham is relying upon his own experience. Lawson, Philip's artist friend who will accompany him to Italy, is, as Richard Cordell has observed, modeled after Sir Gerald Kelly,[12] Maugham's lifelong friend and painter of several portraits of him. And the reputation and behavior of Ruth Chalice, who will go with them on this journey, so closely parallels that of Sue Jones (with whom Maugham has just ended a frustrating eight years) that there can be little doubt that she is a model for the character. The narrator tells the reader:

They did not wish to leave the starlit night, and the three of them would sit on the terrace of Ruth Chalice's room, silent, hour after hour, too tired to talk any more, but in voluptuous enjoyment of the stillness. They listened to the murmur of the river. The church clock struck one and two and sometimes three before they could drag themselves to bed. Suddenly Philip became aware that Ruth Chalice and Lawson were lovers. He divined in it the way the girl looked at the young painter, and in his air of possession; and as Philip sat with them he felt a kind of effluence surrounding them, as though the air were heavy with something strange. The revelation was a

shock. He had looked upon Miss Chalice as a very good fellow and he liked
to talk to her but it never seemed to him possible to enter into a close relationship. (OHB, 247–48)

This relationship, then, is one that Maugham knew well from experience and could therefore portray with credibility. The character of
Ruth Chalice also anticipates Mildred, who is equally free with her
affections, and to whom Philip will have a hopeless bondage of passion. Philip at this point is so envious of Lawson's love that he wishes
"that he was standing in his shoes and feeling with his heart. . . .
fear seized him that love would pass him by." Philip wishes for "a
passion to seize him, he wanted to be swept off his feet and burn
powerlessly in a mighty rush he cared not whither" (OHB, 248). And
of course Philip's wish will be too fully granted.

Returning from Italy, Philip resumes his study of art. He begins
to doubt his ability. Then he remembers Fanny Price—whom he has
not seen since returning—and her strength of will: "If I thought I
wasn't going to be really good, I'd rather give up painting. . . . I
don't see any use in being a second-rate painter." And one morning
he receives a letter.

Please come at once when you get this. I couldn't put up with it any more.
Please come yourself. I can't bear the thought that anyone else should touch
me. I want you to have everything.

F. Price

I have not had anything to eat for three days (OHB, 256)

When Philip finds her she "was hanging with a rope round her neck,
which she had tied to a hook in the ceiling fixed by some previous
tenant to hold up the curtains of the bed. She had moved her own
little bed out of the way and had stood on a chair, which had been
kicked away. It was lying on its side on the floor. They cut her down.
The body was quite cold" (OHB, 257). Realizing that she loved him,
Philip is haunted not only by this portrait of failure and futile determination, but also by her bondage to passion, passion for art and for
him.

Bondage to Mildred

Mildred is a waitress in the A.B.C. tea shop Philip and other medical students at St. Luke's Hospital often frequent. Despite her rather unattractive appearance Mildred becomes more and more the object of Philip's interest. When she first speaks to him, he is elated. He draws a picture of Mildred and gives it to her. He even works up his courage enough to ask her to a play. Her indifferent acceptance will be repeated many times during their relationship: "I don't mind." And after the evening out she continues to react in the same cold manner:

> "I hope you've enjoyed yourself?"
> "Rather."
> "Will you come out with me again one evening?"
> "I don't mind." (*OHB,* 306)

This coldness continues through these early days of their relationship.

> "I say, I do awfully want to call you Mildred."
> "You may if you like, I don't care."
> "And you'll call me Philip, won't you?"
> "I will if I can think of it. It seems more natural to call you Mr. Carey. . . ."
> "Won't you kiss me goodnight?" he whispered.
> "Impudence!" she said. (*OHB,* 313)

Finally Philip appeals to her: "I say, don't be beastly with me, Mildred. You know I'm awfully fond of you. I think I love you with all my heart" (*OHB,* 315). He soon realizes how helpless he has become: "He wanted passionately to get rid of the love that obsessed him; it was degrading and hateful. He must prevent himself from thinking of her. In a little while the anguish he suffered must grow less" (*OHB,* 318). And it is when he becomes aware of his bondage that Philip recalls the bondage that Miss Wilkinson and Fanny Price must have experienced—and Maugham thus clarifies the foreshadowing purpose of those relationships—"His mind went back to the past. He wondered whether Emily Wilkinson and Fanny Price had endured on his account anything like the torment that he suffered now. He felt a pang of remorse." And even here Maugham dramatizes Philip's remorse with the approximation of the sound of his voice: "I didn't know then what it was like, he said to himself" (*OHB*, 318).

Philip therefore becomes increasingly aware of his bondage to Mildred. And Maugham provides the parallel bondage of Mildred to Griffiths, Philip's friend who had nursed him back to health during a recent illness.

"It's not worth while sacrificing everything for an infatuation that you know can't last. After all, he doesn't care for anyone more than ten days, and you're rather cold; that sort of thing doesn't mean very much to you."

"That's what you think."

And even though Philip is unable to exercise reason about his own bondage, he is able to understand Mildred's: "If you're in love with him you can't help it. I'll just bear it the best I can" (*OHB*, 410). The incompatible relationship is here again evident and the one who loves most is victimized:

"Are you awfully unhappy?"

"I wish I was dead," she moaned. "I wish I'd died when the baby came [by Miller, her earlier love]."

And Philip reflects to her: " 'It is awful, love, isn't it?' he said. 'Fancy anyone wanting to be in love' " (*OHB*, 415). Later Mildred replies: "I'm sick with love for him. I know it won't last, just as well as he does . . ." (*OHB*, 416).

At this point Philip portrays behavior that can only be termed masochist:

"Why don't you go away with him?"

"How can I? You know we haven't got the money."

"I'll give you the money." (*OHB*, 416)

Later Philip is able to see more clearly and rationally the parallel between his situation and Mildred's. He admits that trying to force Mildred to love him was attempting the impossible: "He did not know what it was that passed from a man to a woman, from a woman to a man, and made one of them a slave: it was convenient to call it the sexual instinct; but if it was no more than that, he did not understand why it should occasion so vehement an attraction to one person rather than another" (*OHB*, 429). He had not after all attracted

Mildred sexually. Nothing he did seemed to influence her: "Because Mildred was indifferent to him he had thought her sexless; her anemic appearance and thin lips, the body with its narrow hips and flat chest, the languor of her manner, carried out his supposition; and yet she was capable of sudden passions which made her willing to risk everything to gratify them" (*OHB*, 429). He was puzzled by Mildred's attraction to Miller and Griffith, both of whom had no permanent attraction to her. But beyond this position of imbalance and of being the victim, there is a similar tendency in both Mildred and Philip toward masochism:

He tried to think out what those two men had which so strangely attracted her. They both had a vulgar facetiousness which tickled her simple sense of humour, and a certain coarseness of nature; but what took her perhaps was the blatant sexuality which was their most marked characteristic. She had a genteel refinement which shuddered at the facts of life, she looked upon the bodily functions as indecent, she had all sorts of euphemisms for common objects, she always chose an elaborate word as more becoming than a simple one: the brutality of these men was like a whip on her thin white shoulders, and she shuddered with voluptuous pain. (*OHB*, 429)

It amuses Philip that his friends, observing his expressionless face, think him strong-minded and deliberate:

They thought him reasonable and praised his common sense; but he knew that his placid expression was no more than a mask, assumed unconsciously, which acted like the protective colouring of butterflies; and himself was astonished at the weakness of his will. . . . when passion seized him he [like Mildred] was powerless. He had no self-control. He merely seemed to possess it because he was indifferent to many of the things which moved other people. (*OHB*, 430)

In the final stages of Philip's bondage he comes to conclusions about the meaning of life and relationships. After Mildred leaves with Griffiths, a relationship that is certain to fail, Philip does not see her again for some time. When one day he happens to see her on the street, "His heart stood still. He saw Mildred. He had not thought of her for weeks. . . . his heart beating excitedly he followed her. He did not wish to speak to her, but he wondered where she was going at that hour; he wanted to get a look at her face" (*OHB*, 495). Of course, he soon learns that she has taken up prostitution. Philip talks to her, learns that the baby is being taken care of, that she must walk the streets to survive. He wants to help. He wants to take care of her. Taking her and the baby to his own apartment, Philip spends pleasant days taking care of them. The end of these days comes when Philip, after prolonged suffering and pain, realizes that he can exercise reason and thereby free himself of the passion that bound him.

"I do love you, Philip," she said.
"Don't talk damned rot. . . ."
"It isn't, it's true. I can't live without you. I want you. . . . I love you Philip. I want to make up for all the harm I did you. I can't go on like this, it's not in human nature. . . ."
"I'm very sorry, but it's too late. . . ."
"But why? How can you be so cruel?"
"I suppose it's because I loved you too much. I wore the passion out." (*OHB*, 537)

Enraged, Mildred finally shouts: "Cripple" (*OHB*, 539).

Freedom From Bondage

Philip's relationship with Sally is significant for the novel and as a reflection of Maugham's life. The daughter of Mr. Athelny, a friend whom Philip met while working, Sally is the oldest daughter of a large family. Their relationship develops quite naturally during Philip's frequent visits to the Athelny home.

He liked to see her deft movements, and she watched him too now and then with that maternal spirit of hers which was so amusing and yet so charming. He was clumsy at first [he is helping her with the sewing], and she laughed at him. When she bent over and showed him how best to deal with a whole line their hands met. He was surprised to see her blush. (*OHB*, 665)

There is a calmness about this relationship that contrasts sharply with his tense relationship with Mildred.

Philip's evaluation of his relationship with Sally, both as a reflection of Maugham's life and as yet another attempt for Philip to find meaning in life, is significant. Following an affair with Philip, Sally fears that she is pregnant. He "despised himself, all he had aimed at so long within reach at last, and now his inconceivable stupidity had erected this new obstacle." Like Maugham, Philip longed to travel to have the freedom that comes with realizing one's dreams: to go to Spain, "the land of his heart . . . to be imbued with its spirit, its romance and colour and history and grandeur" (*OHB*, 667). And now "this thing had come." He reasoned (now free from the bondage of passion) that it would be "madness to allow such an accident to disturb the whole pattern of his life. . . . He would do what he could for Sally; he could afford to give her a sufficient sum of money. A strong man would never allow himself to be turned from his purpose. Yet he simply could not. He knew himself" (*OHB*, 678–79). Sally "had trusted him and been kind to him. He simply could not do a thing which, notwithstanding all his reason, he felt was horrible." His wedding present to Sally would then be his high hopes. Philip would sacrifice for her: "Self-sacrifice! Philip was uplifted by its beauty, and all through the evening he thought of it" (*OHB*, 680).

There can be little doubt that at this point in his life Maugham was experiencing some of the same emotions. After being rejected by Sue Jones in 1913, Maugham turned to Syrie Wellcome. As Morgan points out: "On the rebound from Sue Jones, he had found a woman who appeared to worship every word that dropped from his lips. . . . One evening after dinner at a restaurant they went back to her apartment and made love for the first time." This was in 1914. It soon became accepted thereafter that Maugham was her lover.[13]

Admitting that the ending of *Of Human Bondage* was for him personally a "turning my wishes into fiction," Maugham states that for some time he "had amused my imagination with pictures of myself in the married state." Similarly, Philip imagines himself married to Sally: "He pictured to himself the long evenings he would spend with Sally in the cosy sittingroom, the blinds undrawn so that they could watch the sea; he with his books, while she bent over her work, and the shaded lamp made her sweet face more fair. They would talk over the growing child, and when she turned her eyes to his there was in them the light of love" (*OHB*, 680). And even the anxiety associated with a pregnancy (without the benefit of marriage) is paralleled in Maugham's own experience: "The affair escalated when Syrie suggested one day that they should have a baby. . . . Maugham was tempted by this offer. . . ." And despite the fact that Syrie was not yet divorced and had been a mistress to Selfridge, a wealthy London businessman, she argued "so persuasively that Maugham yielded."[14]

The ending of the novel, Maugham states, readers "on the whole have found . . . the least satisfactory part" (*SU*, 190). Of course, the reader is moved to a greater extent and is more thoroughly convinced by the relationship of bondage of many individuals—chiefly Philip for

Mildred—earlier in the novel. But it must not be forgotten that the relationship between Philip and Sally is essential in the general movement of the novel and especially in relation to Philip's search for meaning in life. Even in the imagery of the final scenes of the novel the reader senses Sally's affinity to nature and the fulfillment associated with harvest:

A hop-garden was one of the sights connected with Philip's boyhood and the toast-houses to him the most typical feature of the Kentish scene. It was with no sense of strangeness, but as though he were at home, that Philip followed Sally through the long lines of hops. The sun was bright now and cast a sharp shadow. Philip feasted his eyes on the richness of the green leaves. The hops were yellowing, and to him they had the beauty and the passion which poets in Sicily have found in the purple grape. As they walked along Philip felt himself overwhelmed by the rich luxuriance. A sweet scent arose from the fat Kentish soil, and the fitful September breeze was heavy with the goodly perfume of the hops. (*OHB*, 662–63)

In fact, realizing earlier that life had no intrinsic meaning, he now begins to discover how to accept one's situation in life and to find meaning:

He accepted the deformity which had made life so hard for him; he knew that it had warped his character, but now he saw also that by reason of it he had acquired that power of introspection which had given him so much delight. Without it he would never have had his keen appreciation of beauty, his passion for art and literature, and his interest in the varied spectacle of life. The ridicule and the contempt which had so often been heaped upon him had turned his mind inward and called forth those flowers which he felt would never lose their fragrance. Then he saw that the normal was the rarest thing in the world. Everyone had some defect. . . . They were the helpless instruments of blind chance. He could pardon Griffiths for his treachery and Mildred for the pain she had caused him. They could not help themselves. (*OHB*, 680–81)

When Philip is freed from the anxiety of Sally's possible pregnancy, he discovers that he can *put*, not *find*, meaning in life, can surrender to happiness and accept defeat of his selfish desires to travel and seek adventure:

"I was going to ask you to marry me. . . ."
"I thought p'raps you might, but I shouldn't have liked to stand in your way." . . .

"But don't you want to marry *me*?"
"There's no one else I would marry."
"Then that settles it." (*OHB, 684*)

No longer a victim of passion but exercising his own reason, Philip gives pattern and meaning to a life that has no intrinsic goodness or purpose. Ending the novel with dialogue, Maugham's final description of Trafalgar Square indicates a hopeful future (as no doubt he saw for his own life with Syrie Wellcome and their child, Liza): "Cabs and omnibuses hurried to and fro, and the crowds passed, hastening in every direction, and the sun was shining" (*OHB, 684*).

Chapter Six
Works of Accomplishment

Undoubtedly Maugham's experiences during the composing of *Of Human Bondage and The Land of Promise* had a profound influence upon his outlook on life: they were transformed into the characters, relationships, and values of these works; and they had an influence on his future works and particularly his narrative technique.

But in October 1914 Maugham, "in uniform, crossed the Channel with the ambulances. He left London with a play still running in the West End, [*The Land of Promise*], and with his long autobiographical novel [*Of Human Bondage*] in the hands of his publisher."[1] With the outbreak of the war and with the completion of this major novel, Maugham's life altered dramatically. He wrote of this change: "The war broke out. A chapter of my life had finished. A new chapter began" (*SU,* 190). Undoubtedly Maugham continued to long for and work toward the wished-for relationship with a woman (Syrie in life, Sally in fiction). However, certain counterforces began to exert themselves upon his life. He had had a homosexual affair with John Ellingham Brooks when he was in Heidelberg during his school days. He had had a bitter-sweet relationship (exhilaration in the sense of the Willie and Rosie relationship in *Cakes and Ale;* frustration and humiliation in the sense of the Philip and Mildred relationship in *Of Human Bondage*) with Sue Jones that lasted some eight years and ended in her rejecting his marriage proposal. He had had a relationship with Syrie Wellcome—on the rebound from Sue Jones—that already had little promise of fulfilling Maugham's high expectations. And on the Flanders front in the ambulance corps he met Gerald Haxton, an American who became his secretary and companion.

Following the disappointments with Sue and Syrie and his meeting Gerald Haxton, Maugham's sexual preference would thereafter be clearly homosexual. His affair with Syrie (though it continued and eventually—following the birth of their daughter, Liza, resulted in marriage in 1917) would never be the same. It would eventually end in divorce in 1929. The anxiety of this relationship and the earlier one with Sue would be constant sources of experience for Maugham's writing. This anxiety would be the subject of *Cakes and Ale* in 1930; it would be reflected in *The Razor's Edge* in 1944, and would be a central subject in his final work, "Looking Back," in 1962. More immediately it is reflected in *The Moon and Sixpence,* written and published in the early years of his marriage, 1917–19.

All of these experiences and changes influenced his attitude toward life and art. But what is of importance here is that the attitude Maugham had at this point in his life toward his homosexuality is consistent with his earlier attitude toward his differences—a stammer, lack of fluency in English, poor performance in athletic activities, etc. That is, all of these differences he perceives in terms of his sense of inferiority: as limitations, as weaknesses. The present study cannot, of course, generalize on the subject of the relationship, if there is one, between homosexuality and art; it can, however, note the limitation Maugham *perceived* homosexuality to place on the artist's work. He spoke of his own limitations in terms of sympathies, experiences, not having the emotions of "normal men":

My sympathies are limited. I can only be myself, and partly by nature, partly by the circumstances of my life, it is a partial self. Though I have been in love a good many times I have never experienced the bliss of requited love. I know that this is the best thing that life can offer, and it is a thing that almost all men, though perhaps only for a short time, have enjoyed. I have most loved people who cared little or nothing for me, and when people have loved me I have been embarrassed. . . . I have been jealous of my independence. I am incapable of complete surrender. (*SU,* 77)

These statements, as noted in a previous chapter, Maugham published in 1938 in *The Summing Up.* They are yet another instance in which Maugham betrays his sense of inferiority, particularly related to his loves and friendships. His rejection by Sue Jones occurred in 1913 (ending an affair that began in 1906); his meeting of Syrie Wellcome in 1911, his marriage to her in 1917, his divorce in 1929; his meeting Gerald Haxton in 1914. Maugham goes on to say: "And so, never having felt some of the fundamental emotions of normal men it is impossible that my work should have the intimacy, the broad human touch and the animal serenity which the greatest writers alone can give." It seems obvious, therefore, that Maugham perceived his life and art as limited. And here he avoids—as he would throughout his life—mentioning his homosexuality. But more important than

what he says here on this subject is his consistency. He always has
the same attitude toward inferiority: seeing difference as limitation
and weakness—to the point of self-deprecation and even at times
masochism.

If we consider statements he made about El Greco three years earlier in *Don Fernando,* then the nature of this perceived limitation can
be further clarified:

Not long ago I came across the suggestion, made in a ribald spirit, that El
Greco was homosexual. I thought it worth considering. . . . I have suggested that talent consists in an individual way of seeing the world combined with a natural aptitude for creation and that genius is talent with a
greater capacity and a universal sympathy. Now it cannot be denied that the
homosexual has a narrower outlook on the world than the normal man. In
certain respects the natural responses of the species are denied to him. Some
at least of the broad and typical human emotions he can never experience.
However subtly he sees life he cannot see it whole.[2]

Again it must be emphasized that it is Maugham's attitude and perception that is of highest importance—not the subject itself—be it
Maugham's homosexuality or stammering or being orphaned or not
receiving a university education.

As paradoxical as it may seem, his feelings of inferiority and deep
sense of difference from other human beings served as a great source
of inspiration for Maugham's writings. For it was these limitations
that called forth his courage to compensate for what he considered his
weaknesses, to transform his feeling of being an outsider (in all the
ways he sensed this separateness) into a strength. Using all his skill
and experience as a playwright, Maugham exploits the outsider, passive point of view. He habitually saw life from a distance, was passive, and tended to remain aloof—all a part of his unique means of
coping with his differences.

No doubt this passive posture enabled him to observe, to analyze,
to criticize in ways that a more active participant in life could not.
Accordingly, this detached position would make it possible for him
to see the incongruities of human relationships, to be involved more
intellectually than emotionally, to be satirical. Standing outside he
could more easily observe the foibles and weaknesses of others. It is
little wonder that his stylistic tendency was toward the comic and
satiric. In his writings he came more and more to depend upon observations he had made and less upon the experiences that had fueled
his early works—most notably *Of Human Bondage.* Although in one

sense this tendency limited his portrayal of characters (for instance, the Gauguin painter in Charles Strickland of *The Moon and Sixpence* and the mystic Larry Darrell of *The Razor's Edge*), Maugham developed this limitation into a strength by creating a distinctively Maughamian dramatized first-person narrator (nowhere more effective than in *Cakes and Ale*—in which the character portrayal of Rosie is especially strong). He saw life from a greater distance, and exploited his dramatic capabilities—for a while in drama and then in fiction. Like Robert Browning, who turned from drama to poetry and created the dramatic monologue, Maugham turned from drama to fiction and created the dramatized first-person narrator. Gradually learning the potential of this device as it suited his experience, outlook, and talents, Maugham eventually would refine it to a point that would enable him to appeal to and involve his readers in ways—certainly unusual for traditional narrative—comparable to that of the more innovative stream of consciousness/interior monologue techniques being used by certain of his contemporaries.

Dramatized Narrator

Using this dramatized first-person narrator in *The Moon and Sixpence* (1919)—for the first time since *The Making of a Saint* (1898)—Maugham only partially realized its potential. It did offer objectivity—the action being seen from a detached, external narrator—which was a key to the success of *Of Human Bondage,* and it did involve the reader: not forcing a conclusion upon the reader (as Hardy often does), allowing the reader to ascertain a meaning for himself or herself. Second, it provided a means of gaining greater distance from issues and experiences, of taking on the perspective of the observer, a friend whose curiosity drives him, a confidant of those directly involved, an observer who, like the reader, is outside the main action. But unlike later Maughamian narrators, this one in *The Moon and Sixpence* is, as Robert Calder states, "youthfully priggish, rather stiff and self-conscious, the ease and mellowness of the later persona are not present. . . ."[3]

In this novel the narrator initially tells the reader that he found nothing unusual about Charles Strickland, the English stockbroker whom he first met at Mrs. Strickland's society parties and who would later be known as one of the great painters of the day. When Strickland left England for Paris and left wife and children behind with only a note of farewell, everyone—especially his wife, Amy—was certain that he had left them for another woman. In fact, they were so certain that they pressed the narrator, who is never given a name in the novel, into going over to Paris with the mission of discovering who she was and convincing Strickland that the only sensible thing for him to do was to return to his homeland and to his wife and family now that he had had his middle-age fling. But when the narrator arrived, he discovered that Strickland was living in a very humble hotel, had no woman living with him and was interested in none, and had a passion only to paint. Returning with this news, the narrator was met first with unbelief and then with indifference. Soon Mrs. Strickland goes into business to support herself and her family and surprisingly does quite well. Although knowing the truth now, she nevertheless allows others the impression that she is a wronged woman, hurt by the fickleness of the male. Several years later the narrator sees Strickland in Paris and makes the acquaintance of another painter, Dick Stroeve, who, while having little talent for painting, has genuine ability as an art critic. He sees genius in Strickland's painting. He presses his wife, Blanche, to tend to Strickland when he is ill, urges Strickland to use his own studio, and even provides Blanche as a model. When Strickland has a love affair with his wife, Stroeve makes no objection—content to be serving the high ideals of art and the needs of a great artist. And when Strickland is finished painting Blanche, he is finished with her.

But before Strickland completes his painting Stroeve exhibits the ambivalent emotions of a Philip Carey, drawn to and yet repelled by the love object, fascinated and at times even enjoying the experience. In light of this masochistic type behavior, it is interesting to recall Maugham's own statement about himself: "I have most loved [those] who cared little . . . for me" (SU, 77). Stroeve insists upon being the one to leave their lodging so that Blanche and Strickland can live there in comfort. And, as Philip did for Mildred, he gives Blanche money as he leaves, half of all he has. Later, he even follows her through the street—suffering all the time. And when she discovers him, she slaps him soundly across the face—perhaps feeding his masochism. Soon afterward Blanche takes acid and dies. Stroeve then discovers the nude painting that Strickland had done of her. As painful as it is to view that work, the art critic in him wins out: it is truly a great work of art, he concludes, with obvious pleasure.

But Strickland is indifferent to it all. He ventures to Tahiti where he paints with no concern for the safety of his works. He is be-

friended at a hotel by Tiare, a woman hotel keeper, who even finds
him a native wife, Ata. Three of his happiest years Strickland spends
with Ata, who, like other Maugham characters embodying wished-
for relationships (e.g., Sally in *Of Human Bondage*), expects little of
him, loves him, and is sensitive to his needs. Strickland paints, while
Ata and their baby place few demands upon him. When a doctor
comes one day to their hut, he discovers that Strickland has become
a leper. Only Ata stays as Strickland furiously paints, trying to complete his masterpiece on the walls of his hut. But when it is finished,
he swears Ata to secrecy and demands that she burn it all down when
he dies. Later the narrator returns to England and visits Amy. She
now speaks highly of her husband's talents, and she speaks proudly
of her own collection of his works.

Two observations can therefore be made about this important work
in Maugham's career. First, in it he has returned to the dramatized
first-person narrator that he last used in *The Making of a Saint* (1898),
now employing, of course, all the lessons learned from his dramatic
apprenticeship and also those learned from his early mistakes—the
verbose style, the overly complicated and demanding plot of *The
Making of a Saint,* and the excessively metaphoric and decorative style
of *The Land of the Blessed Virgin.*

Also, through the use of the dramatized first-person narrative technique, Maugham is able to achieve an effect similar to that in *Of Human Bondage*—objectivity of presentation, lack of a conventional
moral or message. Furthermore, this technique allows the reader to
remain relatively free to experience the narrative and to draw conclusions—influenced, of course, by the rather undogmatic, objective,
cynical, and somewhat amoral Maughamian narrator.

Second, in *The Moon and Sixpence* Maugham has learned to work
within his limitations, to draw from his observations and experiences
as a source for his material. In other words, he has discovered a way
of writing that best suits his talents. He has already learned to write
simply and in a plain style. And he has learned to write depending
less upon his imagination and more upon his own experiences and
observations. Accordingly, *The Moon and Sixpence* takes up a subject
of growing concern to Maugham, namely, the relationship between
an artist's life and his or her art. This concerns Maugham obviously
because he had always attempted to design his life the way an artist
designs an artwork. But there is another important dimension to the
life-and-art subject in this work. Granted that Maugham's interest in

art, and his interest in Gauguin's art in particular, was an influence in his choices of material for this novel. He had had time—having first visited Tahiti in 1916 and having become fascinated with Gauguin—to put his observation on art and Gauguin into perspective. But a major concern of the novel is the relative priority that an artist places upon his art—compared with more materialistic concerns and with human relationships, especially the relationship between the artist and his or her spouse, the relationship between a man and a woman. In this way, then, his present concerns—as had been true for *Of Human Bondage*—became important in the dynamics of the composing process for him and became a major source of material for this novel. That is, Maugham's *present concern* during the writing of this work, 1917–19, was his unhappy marriage to Syrie. He experienced the feelings of ambivalence that are typical of the psychology of an individual in such a situation: drawn to Liza, his daughter, and to the comfort and respectability of the married state, but drawn also to Gerald Haxton, his male lover, to travel and adventure, and drawn, above all, to his art. And, as with Charles Strickland, art wins out—for his work, for his career as a writer, everything and everyone must be sacrificed.

But however close *The Moon and Sixpence* may be to *Of Human Bondage* in its objectivity and method of involving the reader, it falls short in depending more upon observation than experience. Certainly Maugham was experiencing the dilemma of dedication to art and work versus dedication to wife, child, duty—as was Strickland. And that dimension of the novel is no doubt what readers remember most vividly. But when the reader moves to a consideration of Strickland as genius/artist, he or she is kept outside, never allowed into the consciousness—let alone the mind—of such an artistic genius.

But the success of *The Moon and Sixpence* testifies in many ways to the quality of the material that Maugham drew from the sources of observation and experience, as well as his ability to dramatize his life in fiction. Maugham continued to write plays and to draw from the same sources for material and to perfect the objective stance—staying outside, stopping short of an in-depth probing, exploiting the comic mode. Of his plays he says:

They were written in the tradition which flourished so brightly in the Restoration period, which was carried on by Goldsmith and Sheridan, and which, since it has had so long a vogue may be supposed to have something in it that peculiarly appeals to the English temper. . . . [the comedy of manners] treats with indulgent cynicism the humours, follies and vices of the world of fashion. It is urbane, sentimental at times, for that is in the English character, and a trifle unreal. It does not preach; sometimes draws a moral, but with a shrug of the shoulders as if to invite you to lay not too great a stress on it.[4]

Comedy of Society

There is no doubt that Maugham had drawn upon his observations of the superficiality, pretentiousness, and hypocrisy of the Mayfair society he knew in London from 1908 (the date of his first theatrical success and beginning of the dinner invitations) to 1915 (the year that he wrote *Our Betters* and the year *Of Human Bondage* was published). But the portrait of unfaithfulness, the lack of loyalty, the misplaced values, and the unhappiness of marriage spring in large part from Maugham's actual and anticipated experience rather than from his observation. He was involved in an affair that would result in an unhappy marriage, was well aware of Syrie's previous unfaithfulness, and conscious that she had most recently been a mistress to Selfridge—an individual very much like the character Arthur Fenwick, and she was very much like Lady Grayson in *Our Betters*.[5] Thus, he transferred many of these anxieties and emotions of his present life into this play.

Written in 1916 in Rome—near the time of the birth of his daughter Liza[6]—though not performed until 1917 in New York and 1923 in London, *Our Betters* portrays Americans in London society, expatriates making their way up the social ladder with little regard for the needs and feelings of others and above all denying their backgrounds in America. Bessie Saunders is a young American who has recently come to London to visit her elder sister Lady Grayson. The elder sister is established in society and Bessie idolizes her. Bessie ignores her sister's unfaithfulness to Lord Grayson and her flirtatious affair with Arthur Fenwick, a wealthy American businessman. But when, during a party, Lady Grayson allows passion to overcome her and ventures off to the tea house to have sex with Tony Paxton, another society woman's kept man, Bessie is disillusioned and determines to return to America. Reminiscent of Congreve's *The Way of the World,* the following exchange captures much of the displaced values of this society:

> CLAY: Did you ever know her husband?
>
> PEARL: Oh yes, I met him. Just the ordinary little Dago. I cannot imagine why she should ever have been in love with him. She's an extraordinary creature. D'you know I'm convinced that she's never had an affair.
>
> CLAY: Some of these American women are strangely sexless.
>
> FLEMING: I have an idea that some of them are even virtuous.
>
> PEARL: [*With a smile.*] It takes all sorts to make a world. (*CP,* 3:16)

Finally Bessie realizes the nature of this world that so attracted her at first: "I've been blind and foolish. Because I was happy and having a good time, I never stopped to ask for explanations of this, that and the other. I never thought. . . . The life was so gay and brilliant—it never struck me that underneath it all . . ." (*CP,* 3:108).

Of course, Maugham knew firsthand much of the nature of London literary and social life. It was there that he met Sue Jones and Syrie Wellcome. Subsequently the war changed Maugham's life. He would return to London society and for a time live with his wife and daughter in Mayfair, but he would never be at home there and would divorce in 1929, purchase a villa on the French Riviera, and spend the rest of his life there (with the exception of the World War II years in America), away from English society.[7]

The reception of *Our Betters* was understandably rather mixed. Negative reactions ranged from calling it bitter[8] and overtly immoral[9] to "acrid comedy" and a banal story.[10] Other reviews were more balanced in their criticism, with some praise for the play: the *New York Dramatic Mirror,* for instance, called it "brilliant satire," but "morally sordid" and "offensive' with too much attention to "human decay." And yet, the reviewer added, it has cleverly cynical dialogue.[11] And Channing Pollock in the *Green Book Magazine* called attention to its wit and "clinical cleverness," while noting that its brilliance was "the brilliance of decay. It is hard and cynical and pitiless."[12]

Both *Our Betters* and *Of Human Bondage,* then, show the influence of Maugham's life upon his works. A similar working out of tensions and dilemmas would inspire his writings of the years to follow. Not long after Maugham met Gerald Haxton and after the birth of his daughter Liza, Maugham agreed to marry Syrie when her divorce was final. But before doing so, he left in 1916 on a trip to Tahiti to gather material for his writing, picking up Gerald Haxton in Chicago to accompany him. On this trip, of course, he discovered much of the material for *The Moon and Sixpence,* as well as that for numerous short stories, most notably those in the collection entitled *The Trembling of a Leaf,* published in 1921 and dedicated to his close friend Bertram Alanson. And one story in particular in this collection (the first short stories he had written in over twenty years) would prove especially popular with readers, and would become a popular play: "Rain," based upon his observations during this voyage. When Maugham returned in 1917, he and Syrie were married as planned— a marriage of convenience for both of them, it no doubt seemed the reasonable thing to do.

Comedy of Marriage

It was also during this period, 1917–19, that Maugham wrote *The Circle,* although it was not performed until 1921. Perhaps his most popular comedy, it focuses upon two relationships: an older couple who thirty years ago gave up everything for romantic love; and a young couple who are now deciding to take a similar course of action. Despite the warnings of the older couple—Lady Kitty (who left her husband, Clive Champion-Cheney) and Lord Porteous—the young couple—Elizabeth (Lady Kitty's daughter-in-law) and Edward Lutton—decide to risk everything for love. Unable to learn from those who are experienced, they seemingly must make their own mistakes. And in so doing, their emotions win out over their reason.

Arnold, Kitty's son and a promising politician, has made a hobby of interior decorating (the profession of Maugham's wife, Syrie, of course) and is nervous as the play opens because his father, Clive Champion-Cheney, is arriving from abroad at the exact time that his mother and her husband are to arrive. Arnold's wife Elizabeth urges him to treat his mother and her husband, Lord Porteous, kindly despite the fact that he has never forgiven his mother for eloping thirty years ago. At first Arnold is adamant in his condemnation of his mother. But Elizabeth pleads her case well:

> ARNOLD: My dear Elizabeth, it's no good going over all that
> again. The facts are lamentably simple. She had a hus-
> band who adored her, a wonderful position, all the

> money she could want, and a child of five. And she ran
> away with a married man. . . .

ELIZABETH: Perhaps your mother couldn't help herself—if she was in
> love? . . . Some of us are more mother and some of us
> more woman. It gives me a little thrill when I think
> that she loved that man so much. She sacrificed her
> name, her position and her child to him. (*CP*, 4:9).

But the tensions increase. When Arnold's father enters, it is Elizabeth who tells him that his ex-wife and her husband are soon to arrive. And he agrees to help minimize the awkwardness of the
situation.

At this point, Teddie, a planter in Malaya, declares his love for
Elizabeth. And even though she is married to Arnold, she admits her
love for him. When Lady Kitty arrives, everything is in confusion.
She mistakes Teddie for Arnold. And in the midst of it all, Clive
enters to make matters even worse.

Teddie urges Elizabeth to leave for Malaya with him the next day.
And later when she and Arnold quarrel, she admits that she is in love
with Teddie. Predictably, Arnold flies into a rage and orders Teddie
to leave immediately.

But Clive gives his son Arnold advice on how to handle the problem. When Clive shows Kitty a picture of herself thirty-five years before, she bursts into tears. He presses his point and urges Kitty to
persuade Elizabeth not to make the mistake of eloping with Teddie.
But when Arnold, on the advice of his father, offers Elizabeth her
freedom—hoping, of course, to prevent her from leaving—she jumps
at the chance. Like Kitty and Porteous thirty years before, she and
Teddie rush into the unknown, risking everything for the passion of
love.

On the whole *The Circle* was received favorably by the critics. The
Dramatist praised its brilliant dialogue; the *Graphic* its "witty, sardonic lines," finding it "very entertaining";[13] and the *New York World*
recognized it as the "best piece of writing" that Maugham had done
for the stage.[14] Frank Swinnerton in the *Nation and the Athenaeum*
termed it the work of a "sentimentalist turned cynic," and while
finding the situation well prepared and treated with great skill, noted
a conflict between sentimentality and cynicism. The result, he further
observed, was to make the characterization uncertain and to rob the

play of its unity. As an example he pointed to Maugham's handling of Arnold: at one time a "fussy fool" and at another an "injured gentleman."[15] Far from seeing the cynicism of the play as a problem, Desmond MacCarthy in the *New Statesman* took the position that Maugham's writing improves in merit and interest as he continues to write from a cynical point of view. By cynical he meant "skeptical with regard to depth and persistence of human affection." He concludes that *The Circle* is one of Maugham's best and one of his most cynical. He does lodge two objections: Lord Porteous is "conventionally drawn and commonplace and uninteresting"; and Maugham exhibits an insensitivity to feeling and language as shown in occasional "vulgar phrases."[16] The *Saturday Review* critic found all of Maugham's good qualities in this play: smartness of dialogue, sense of a situation, and skill at indicating character. But Robert Allerton Parker, in his "Comedy and Color" in *Arts and Decoration,* captured what Maugham had developed to this point and also what many readers—although attracted to it—found uncomfortable and not as they would wish life to be: "written with a sharp pen, dipped in ink that contains too much acid, and too little of the milk of human kindness."[17]

At the time this work was composed, around 1919, the emotions of Lady Kitty and Lord Porteous are not unlike those that Maugham was experiencing. With Sue Jones, Maugham had had the exciting and youthful—although unconventional—romance that Elizabeth and Teddie feel and that Kitty and Porteous have felt. Like Clive, though, Maugham is not experiencing requited love, and looks on passively while others enjoy mutual love. And by 1919 Maugham's relationship with Syrie was becoming increasingly impossible. Like the relationship between Lord and Lady Grayson in *Our Betters* and Mr. and Mrs. Strickland in *The Moon and Sixpence,* their relationship was more of an appearance than a reality, a way of concealing the truth of their incompatibility. And before Maugham, as before Elizabeth and Teddie, was the possibility of happiness in what seemed then would be a compatible, albeit unconventional relationship (that is, with Gerald Haxton).

Emotions—more than any individuals whom he had known or observed—served as models for these and most of his other works. In fact, the attraction of the South Seas and of foreign cultures with their unique life-styles was consistent with his interests and inclinations at this time in his life.

Conventional and Natural Values

In 1921 Maugham published *The Trembling of a Leaf,* his first collection of short stories since *Orientations* in 1898. Drawing upon the
same anxieties that fed *The Moon and Sixpence,* Maugham wrote "The
Fall of Edward Barnard," treating the theme of a businessman leaving
both his business and his fiancée in Chicago to go to Tahiti to seek
his fortune. Edward, the businessman, plans in this way to prepare
himself for marriage to Isabel, his fiancée, and a successful and happy
life in Chicago society. In the end, like Strickland in *The Moon and
Sixpence,* and like Larry in a later novel, *The Razor's Edge,* Edward rejects standard morality and traditional success in favor of the naturalness and spontaneity of life in Tahiti. When Barnard does not return
in a reasonable time and does not seem himself in his letters, Isabel
sends Bateman—as Amy Strickland in *The Moon and Sixpence* sends
the Maughamian character to inquire after her husband in Paris—to
determine the nature of the situation. And of course he finds that Edward has fallen, has adopted a new code of behavior and new values—
as did Strickland in *The Moon and Sixpence* and Darrell in *The Razor's
Edge.* Confronting Edward with the possibility that his actions will
upset Isabel to the point that she will call off their engagement entirely, Bateman is shocked by Edward's indifferent reaction. Bateman
is so agitated by this attitude that he says to his old friend: "I wish
you had ordinary clothes on. . . . It's such a tremendously serious
decision you're taking. That fantastic costume of yours makes it seem
terribly casual."[18] The contrast in values between these two old
friends is striking. Barnard with his tolerance and understanding falls
short of the fallen person the reader is prepared to see. And Bateman
with his desperate clinging to appearances seems less admirable at
this moment. But characteristically Maugham stops short of weight-
ing the reader's sympathies in either direction; both have strong qualities as well as other, less desirable ones. However, the title of the
short story from this point on becomes ironical. When Bateman reports to Isabel upon his return and, although disappointed, she accepts his proposal for marriage, the contrast is inescapable. Embracing
Bateman, Isabel thinks of the "exquisite house she would have, full
of antique furniture, and of the concerts she would give . . . , and
the dinners to which only the most cultured people would come"
(*TL,* 114). And of course Bateman would be the perfect businessman:

he would "wear horn spectacles." And the story ends with a thought of the fallen Edward Barnard, Isabel sighs: "Poor Edward."

The second short story in this collection that deserves special mention here would be the most popular of all of Maugham's stories, and would become a play (written by John Colton and Clemence Randolph), that ran for 648 performances in New York. Entitled "Rain," it combines Maugham's use of observations and his own tensions and emotions, not unlike what he had done before. But in this work Maugham takes a step further toward the development of a narrative style that would be fully realized in *Cakes and Ale* (1930).

Two couples traveling together on a ship, a missionary and his wife, the Reverend and Mrs. Davidson, and a doctor and his wife, Dr. and Mrs. MacPhail, become traveling friends and begin to feel the intimacy that comes from sharing the common experience of making a journey together. Furthermore, their intimacy is strengthened by the negative reaction they have to others on board—especially the lower class. While their ship to Asia is quarantined in Pago-Pago, they stay in a hotel-store, where one passenger—Sadie Thompson from the Red Light district of Honolulu—becomes the object of their disapproval. She quickly makes her presence known with her drinking, dancing, and loud parties in her room. The reaction of Dr. MacPhail, a medical doctor who, like Maugham, has had experience in the war, differs from the others': less critical of Sadie, more tolerant of others, unapproving of the manner in which the Davidsons force their views on others, and suspicious of his wife's easy acceptance of the views of the Davidsons. Mr. Davidson takes Sadie on as his personal project, to chasten and to reform. But his efforts are so intense that they reveal an unnaturalness; he has obviously repressed so much of his natural desires and emotions that in a moment of weakness he yields to Miss Thompson's physical beauty. As a result of the guilt and remorse he then feels for this violation of his behavior code, the Reverend Davidson commits suicide. The story ends with Sadie Thompson's gramophone now once more loudly playing and her complaining that all men are alike, that all men are beasts.

In this work, then, Maugham has returned to the familiar themes of the hypocrisy of conventional morality, and the joy and essential goodness of many of those whom it condemns. Although not the narrator or a central character, Dr. MacPhail serves to counterbalance the attitude of the traditional view of individuals such as his wife and the Reverend and Mrs. Davidson. Representing much of the Maughamian persona—worldly wise, tolerant, cynical, objective—MacPhail is furthermore like Maugham in that he is a medical doctor and has recently returned from the war.

But the work is not a simple one in which the reader is given all of the information and receives it passively. For one thing, the contrast between Davidson and MacPhail is evident from the beginning, as is MacPhail's obvious admiration for much of what Davidson represents—in many ways Davidson has capabilities that MacPhail lacks.

Dr. MacPhail is a man of forty—the approximate age of Maugham when he made the journey to Tahiti. Characteristically Maugham describes him by a reference to what sets him off from others, his uniqueness or abnormality: "When he sat down under the light and took off his hat you saw that he had very red hair, with a bald patch on the crown," and "with a pinched face, precise and rather pedantic." When he speaks, he speaks in a Scots accent, in a low, quiet voice. But although he is timid, he is "no fool." And he does not take offense easily.

The Reverend Davidson is by nature "reserved and even morose," "a silent, rather sullen man, and you felt that his affability was a duty that he imposed upon himself." He is tall and thin, with hollow cheeks and high cheek bones, full and sensual lips. His dark eyes are set "deep in their sockets . . . large and tragic." His hands are large with "big, long fingers" that are finely shaped, giving "him a look of great strength." He is a man with whom no real intimacy is possible. But the most striking quality of the Reverend Davidson is "the feeling he gave you of suppressed fire" (*TL*, 248–49).

Dr. MacPhail obviously admires the Reverend Davidson, finding him both impressive and troubling. "In the course of all the conversations they had had with Reverend Davidson one thing had shone out clearly and that was the man's unflinching courage" (*TL*, 256). A timid man, Dr. MacPhail never got used to the danger of the war: "operating in an advanced dressing-station the sweat poured from his brow and dimmed his spectacles," and he had to make an effort "to control his unsteady hand":

He shuddered a little as he looked at the missionary.
    "I wish I could say that I've never been afraid," he said.
    "I wish you could say that you believed in God," Rev. Davidson replied, obviously without any fear of embarrassment for his bluntness. (*TL*, 257)

But like the rain that continues while all the characters are powerless to stop it, the "suppressed fire," the natural desires that the Reverend Davidson has so long repressed, must assert itself. His great courage is powerless to control his desires. In fact, this act of desire completes his character although it drives him to suicide. Even Dr. MacPhail grows in the experience: when Sadie Thompson turns her gramophone to full volume, the narrator says: "Dr. MacPhail gasped. He understood" (*TL,* 301).

Changing Sexual Manners

The Constant Wife was a failure in London, mainly because of mismanagement, but a great success in America (where Ethel Barrymore played the lead) and in other countries, as well as in provincial towns in England (*CP,* 4:xix). Brooks Atkinson of the *New York Times* called it a "deft and sparkling comedy . . . written with wit and sprightliness."[19] And Raphael considers it "an amusing though perhaps slightly laborious comedy of changing sexual manners."[20]

In the tradition of his other comedies, the play concerns the manners of society and the hypocrisies and misplaced values of its members. Here Maugham takes up the issue of the double standard and the rights of women, matters of considerable concern at that time and later, of course. It opens with Martha and Mrs. Culver, Constance's sister and mother, considering whether to tell Constance that her husband and her best friend, John and Mary-Louisa, are carrying on a love affair. Deciding to do so, they try to tell Constance what is taking place, but she blocks all of their attempts. And unexpectedly Bernard, Constance's old flame whom she has not seen for years, arrives for a visit. Later Martha meets Bernard and tells him of John's unfaithfulness. As part of the complication of the play, Mary-Louisa fears discovery and nervously telephones John at his work, Martha and Bernard attempt again to alert Constance, Mrs. Culver speaks to Constance with little success, and finally Mortimer, Mary-Louisa's husband, confronts Constance with the unfaithfulness of his wife and her husband. As proof he produces a cigarette case belonging to John that he found in his bedroom. Surprisingly, Constance defends her husband, says that she left the cigarette case there herself during a visit, and challenges him to produce further evidence, which he cannot do. Then, when she has Mary-Louisa and John there, she admits that she has known of their affair all along. Sending Bernard off to put Mary-Louisa in a taxi, she tells John that theirs has been a good marriage, that they both stopped loving the other at the same time, and that she has decided to accept an offer of work that she has recently received—thereby no longer being financially dependent upon him. A year later Constance is preparing to take a long holiday in Italy. Mary-Louisa, now reconciled with Mortimer, has just returned from a trip to India. Martha is curious as to why John is not planning to accompany Constance. And not understanding why he has not been included in the plans, John asks Constance whether he should not go along, insisting at the same time that he has broken off his affair with Mary-Louisa. But Constance refuses to consider his request. Mary-Louisa arrives to speak with Constance about her decision to drop John. Pressing her, Constance discovers that Mary-Louisa's reason for doing so is not disinterested: she has found another man, someone she met on their trip to India. Constance tells Mary-Louisa that she is an immoral beast, not as good as an honest prostitute. Believing that Constance has just told Mary-Louisa of his wish to break off the affair, John returns to ask how she took it. Constance assures him that she took it well. John then offers Constance a check to cover the expenses of her forthcoming trip to Italy, but she refuses. Instead she presents him with a check to cover her board for the past year. Thus declaring her independence, she tells him that as long as she was financially dependent upon him she felt she had no right to condemn him for his affair with Mary-Louisa. She also announces that she is going to Italy to spend the holiday with Bernard, her old flame, with the intention, she says, of being adored before it is too late. Her mother comes in at this point and is simply shocked at her daughter's behavior. John first pleads with her and then threatens to go back to Mary-Louisa. When Constance informs him that Mary-Louisa has found another, he explodes. In only a few moments, though, he admits that while Constance is the most maddening of women, she is also the most delightful. And he agrees to take her back when she returns in six weeks.

The Constant Wife, like his earlier comedies, is critical of conventional morality. In this work Maugham keeps alive his skills of witty dialogue and satiric portrayal of English society. But here Maugham is exploring and transforming emotions and concerns of his own as he and Syrie lived lives that were essentially separate and independent. She, of course, had become a celebrated decorator in London and he had his work, travels, and Gerald Haxton. As Curtis observes, "Syrie's increasing renown in her career caused Maugham to ponder women's lib long before that phrase became current, and to make it the main subject of [this] comedy."[21] Again, as previously observed, such grounding of his work in personal concerns always lends authenticity to Maugham's writings.

Ashenden: "R," "A Domiciliary Visit," "Miss King"

Drawing upon his experience in World War I, Maugham published *Ashenden,* a collection of short stories, in 1926. In his preface Maugham states: "Fact is a poor story-teller. It starts a story at haphazard, generally long before the beginning, rambles on inconsequently and trails off, leaving loose ends hanging about, without conclusion. It works up to an interesting situation, and then leaves it in the air to follow an issue that has nothing to do with the point; it has no sense of climax and whittles away its dramatic effects in irrelevance."[22] These statements, of course, tell us as much about Maugham's views on composing as they do about this particular work. Always his goal was to create a plausible harmony. As he stated in the preface to his 1932 collection of short stories, *East and West:* "I like a story that fits. I did not take to writing stories seriously till I had had much experience as a dramatist, and this experience taught me to leave out everything that did not serve the dramatic value of my story. It taught me to make incident follow incident in such a manner as to lead up to the climax I had in mind."[23]

In his work we see the Maughamian character, here Ashenden, the rather detached observer and participant, progressively developed. Although the stories are presented by an external narrator, the focus throughout is upon Ashenden—as it was upon Philip in *Of Human Bondage.*

"R," the first story, provides the reader with an introduction to the occasion and circumstance by which Ashenden is approached by a colonel, "R" as he is known in the Intelligence Department, and enlisted to go as an English spy to Geneva. Ashenden agrees and all is settled for him to depart. Before leaving him, though, "R" states, "If you do well you'll get no thanks and if you get into trouble you'll get no help" (*A, 3*).

The second story, "A Domiciliary Visit," builds upon "R." Ashenden is living in Geneva and is just returning from France where he

was writing and dispatching a report. When he returns to his hotel
the porter informs him that there are two gentlemen waiting for him
in his room. The visitors he soon learns are policemen who have come
to question him. Aware that they searched his room and are alert to
any mistakes that he might make, Ashenden answers them with care.
In the process of describing the situation and Ashenden's predica-
ment, the narrator gives us considerable information about Ashenden:
"had in him a strain of flippancy"; "was a neat creature" (*A*, 9)—
thereby noticing that his room had been thoroughly searched; "it was
Ashenden's principle . . . always to tell as much of the truth as he
conveniently could . . ." (*A*, 10); "had a confident belief in the stupidity of the human animal . . ."; "was a humorist" (*A*, 12). By
carefully answering their questions, Ashenden "wriggled out of the
fix." If he had been arrested, he "knew his chief well enough to be
aware that when he had told him that if he got into trouble he need
look for no help he meant exactly what he said" (*A*, 18).

"Miss King," the third story, builds further upon these two. It is
in many ways a more substantial work, one that Maugham would
later include in *East and West*. Rather than any action, turn of events,
or intricate plot, it is the character Ashenden that is of greatest significance to this work. A detached observer who participates indirectly in the lives of the other characters, Ashenden places a high
value upon pleasure. The narrator first describes Ashenden in his
bath. The concern over the policemen who have recently questioned
him is lost in the pleasure of the hot bath. With considerable calm
he is now able to consider the greater care he will take in his task of
obtaining instruction and message twice a week from the peasant
woman at the market. But in the midst of his thought, he suddenly
realizes that the water is no longer warm. As he is reaching for the
tap with his hands and unable to turn it with his feet, it occurs to
him that people who believe that he has character have not seen him
in his bath. But he is at that moment interrupted by a knock at the
door and a message, an invitation from Baroness de Higgins to play
bridge after dinner. He sends a message accepting.

When Ashenden enters the dining room he notices that the baroness has already arrived. While waiting for his dinner he takes note
of the presence of Prince Ali, an Egyptian and bitter enemy of the
English. Prince Ali is living with his two daughters, who spend every
night dancing in restaurants. But each evening the daughters dine in
the hotel, chaperoned by Miss King, an elderly English governess.
Although he has tried, Ashenden has never been able to develop any

friendship with her. He has always been snubbed. Once he was shocked to overhear the daughters verbally abusing her and one even slapped her.

Miss King is small, wears a wig, and dresses in gay clothes. She has, Ashenden once heard, not been to England since she was first engaged as a governess by Prince Ali's mother. For some reason Ashenden feels that Miss King dislikes him.

Finished with her meal, the baroness stops at Ashenden's table to tell him how pleased she is that he has accepted her invitation to play bridge and that he should come to her room shortly after his dinner. Typically, Ashenden eats his meal with pleasure and is one of the last to leave the dining room.

When he arrives to play bridge, he is greeted by the baroness, Prince Ali, and his secretary. They compliment him on his novels—although most of them cannot read English—and on his bridge playing—although he knows that he is no better than a second-class player. As they play it occurs to Ashenden that the baroness may be the one responsible for the policemen's visit to his rooms and that this invitation has come only after nothing was discovered by the officers. He wonders also if they were not sounding him out to see if he would sell himself. And he "felt rather than knew that the Prince was an able and astute man." Shortly after midnight, the prince rises from his chair, thereby signaling the end of the evening.

Returning to his room, Ashenden quickly falls asleep. But in what seems no more than five minutes he is awakened by a messenger. Miss King has had a stroke and requested to see Ashenden. Shocked that she would ask for him, he dresses and goes to her room. When he enters she is on the bed. He is amazed by how small she is—no larger than a child. Ashenden reflects that she must be over eighty. Now she cannot speak because of the damage of the stroke. The assistant manager of the hotel becomes concerned about the potential negative publicity from someone dying in the hotel. Ashenden learns that immediately following the stroke Miss King could at first speak and asked for him, even giving his room number. The assistant manager leaves as does the doctor, leaving Ashenden alone with the maid and Miss King. Dismissing the maid for the evening, he sits in the quiet room observing Miss King: "He felt certain then that he saw in those dark eyes a desperate effort to speak. He could not be mistaken. The mind was shaken by desire, but the paralyzed body was incapable of obedience. For her disappointment expressed itself quite plainly, tears came to her eyes and ran down her cheeks. Ashenden took out his handkerchief and dried them" (A, 36). Ashenden wonders why she called for him when there were others from England in the hotel. Perhaps, he speculates, it is because he is a British agent; perhaps at death one is inclined toward patriotism. And although his common sense "protested," he "became strongly convinced that she had some secret that she wished to impart to him"—because he was a spy and would make use of it.

Curious as to what she might say, Ashenden asks Miss King if it has anything to do with the war. Suddenly she makes a movement and her body convulses. Then, "as though by a final desperate effort of will," she raises up in her bed. She utters just one word,—"England," and dies.

Terming Ashenden Maugham's presentation of the "anti-hero spy," Calder points out that throughout he "demonstrates real indifference to his occupation, often being more interested in writing or material comforts."[24] But, as "Miss King" illustrates, Ashenden is not indifferent to others. Having already accepted the position, having just gone on a mission to France, he is questioned by the Geneva police and answers them quite skillfully, plans his future work with increased caution, accepts the bridge invitation (after he has earlier made a special but unsuccessful effort to be friends with Miss King), is congenial with his hostess and her guests, comes to the dying Miss King's room, stays with her (allowing the maid to leave for the night), and is with Miss King to hear her dying word. Such an ending, in which the Maughamian character learns the answer to a question or problem that he has puzzled over, is a familiar pattern in Maugham's fiction (the narrator in The Moon and Sixpence, Dr. MacPhail in "Rain," Willie Ashenden in Cakes and Ale, Mr. Maugham in The Razor's Edge). Despite the fact that Miss King does not take up a friendship with Ashenden the British agent and apparently has not in any way shown great affection for her native country during her years as a governess, in death she speaks the word England, as if thereby giving her a final sense of identity and affirming her significance. The importance of a character's connection to England is, of course, significant for Maugham's English characters living abroad as in The Land of Promise (1913), as well as "The Outstation" (1923). Whether or not the individuals conform to the values of English society, it is in accordance with those values that they judge themselves.

Chapter Seven
Artistic Excellence

Cakes and Ale: The Skeleton in the Cupboard (1930), in many ways the culmination of his development as a writer of fiction, is a work in which Maugham most fully exploits the abilities that he had refined in his long career. A comic novel in the satiric tradition, it was always Maugham's personal favorite among his novels. Richard Cordell ranks it with *The Moon and Sixpence* and *Of Human Bondage* as his best novels, praises it for its construction and timing, and describes it as "superbly written, ingenious in construction, with well drawn characters and expert use of the colloquial style."[1] Calling it an "essentially humorous novel" and a "satirical-romance," Anthony Curtis notes its "perfection of humourous timing," which he maintains Maugham learned as a playwright, and gives high praise to the style, which he believes "conforms with the utmost quiet and decorum to Dryden's definition of good prose as the conversation of gentlemen. . . ."[2] And Robert Calder finds it to be technically and stylistically Maugham's best work.

Of Maugham's many accomplishments in this novel—the use of comic devices, the completion of the compensation pattern (as traced in the earlier chapters), the blending of both dialogue and nonverbal communication (no doubt growing out of his experiences as a dramatist), and the development of the Maughamian persona (beyond his earlier uses of it)—are especially noteworthy. In this work Maugham carries out a pattern of compensation in terms of his artistic principles (accomplishing and valuing simplicity, clarity, and naturalness in writing which he could not in oral discourse) and in the dramatic narrator (endowing him with qualities he wished for in his own character and relations with others). Furthermore, as part of this pattern of creating in fiction instead of life, Maugham combines in this novel the two major sources of his fictional material: observed and experienced reality.

But the most important development, the major link in the works from *Of Human Bondage* to *Cakes and Ale,* is Maugham's growth as a dramatic writer of fiction. With *The Moon and Sixpence* he had made use of a dramatized first-person narrator, however little developed as a character it may have been, to involve the reader. And in subsequent short stories, particularly in *Ashenden,* he made more extensive use of this dramatic technique. It was possible then for Maugham—with his growing reading public—to draw together in *Cakes and Ale* many of the distinctive characteristics and attitudes of this narrator.

A Comic Novel

The novel concerns itself with the life of a famous novelist, Edward Driffield, and his first wife, Rosie.[3] At the beginning of the novel, Amy, Driffield's second wife, has commissioned Alroy Kear, a popular novelist of the day, to write a biography of her late husband. Willie Ashenden, also a novelist and the narrator of *Cakes and Ale,* has been asked to supply information about the early life of Edward and Rosie—since he knew them from his boyhood days in the late nineteenth century. Meeting them was Willie's introduction to the world of literature. And it was at this time that he first became aware of Rosie's great beauty. He was also impressed with her openness and her kindness to everyone. He and Rosie often went out for dinner and then to the theater. One evening they returned to Willie's apartment and Rosie spent the night. He became her lover.

Returning to his room one evening, Willie Ashenden finds a message from Alroy Kear requesting that he give him a call. Suspecting that Roy wants a favor, Ashenden is in no hurry to contact him. And when he finally does, what he suspected is true: Roy wants help. Since he has been asked to write the Driffield biography, he needs information about Edward and Rosie. But more than that he needs help solving the biggest problem of all: what to do about Rosie, the first wife, who was unfaithful to Edward, who some say was a nymphomaniac, and who ran away with George Kemp to America. Truly, she is for Roy what the subtitle suggests: "The Skeleton in the Cupboard."

After his first meeting with Roy and anticipating a weekend trip with him to Amy Driffield's home in Blackstable, Willie begins to recall details and emotions from his boyhood with Rosie and Edward: home from school for the holiday, the fifteen-year-old Ashenden was warned by his uncle, vicar of Blackstable, not to associate with the wrong people. His aunt and even Mary Ann, their maid, are equally supportive of this restriction. But Willie had a new bicycle and the very couple, Edward and Rosie, who were kind enough to teach him to ride it turned out to be the wrong kind of people—at least in his uncle and aunt's eyes. And despite their disapproval, Willie spent many pleasurable days with the Driffields. But all that came to an end one day when they moved away—without telling anyone and without paying their bills.

Willie next met the Driffields in London during the years of his medical schooling. When he first met Rosie in the street he was reluctant to be friendly because of what he then considered their disgraceful departure from Blackstable. But their friendliness and good humor soon won him over and he became a regular guest at their home, meeting writers and artists and occasionally individuals of considerable social position—at least for those days. Soon Willie and Rosie became lovers. For sometime thereafter he suspected Rosie of having love affairs with others, but was reluctant to admit to himself that this was actually happening. When he confronted her, she admitted it openly and urged him to accept her as she is. Willie could not resist her genuineness. But shortly thereafter Rosie left London for America with George Kemp.

So, when Alroy Kear and Amy Driffield pressure Willie Ashenden for information about Rosie and Edward and about those early days in Blackstable, he is forced to be selective. Much to their displeasure he continually insists that Rosie was always good and kind and generous. As a result, then, rather than having his problem solved, Roy finds himself faced with a larger dilemma. On the one hand, he can paint a true picture of Rosie's important role in Edward's life: the influence that inspired his best works. On the other hand, he can please Amy by drawing a picture of Rosie that is as negative as the one of Edward is positive. Neither, obviously, is satisfactory.

Ironically Rosie is not dead as Roy and Amy have assumed. And shortly after his meeting with them, Willie sees her in New York. Now over seventy, she is the same warm and loveable person he knew years before. Still curious about her motivation for running way with George Kemp, Willie inquires about her reasons. Rosie says that she and Edward never got over the death of their six-year-old daughter who died of meningitis. She tells of the night George came to her broken by a financial misfortune, pleading for her to go with him. Rosie simply could not refuse. But to the question of what she ever saw in George she replies, much to Willie's amazement, "He was always such a perfect gentleman."

Comedy in Fiction

Shortly after the publication of *Cakes and Ale,* Maugham sent a copy to Paul Dottin, a French scholar and teacher and the first literary critic to take Maugham's works seriously.[4] In the accompanying letter Maugham informs Dottin that he is sending the copy with the wish that he read it since the novel represents a new style for him, a change that his readers seem to be enjoying.[5]

One could speculate that the new style Maugham refers to is the development of the Maughamian persona, or the blending of dialogue and nonverbal communication. One could see the completion of the compensation pattern or his drawing upon observed and experienced sources as the distinctiveness of the style in this novel. Or one could look to the character Rosie as combining what Ward[6] has called the two types of female characters in Maugham's writing: the mother figure (Miss Ley in *Mrs. Craddock;* Sally in *Of Human Bondage*) and the *hetaira* figure, the female whose appearance and manner causes men to become sexually aroused (Guilia in *The Making of a Saint;* Mildred in *Of Human Bondage*). None of these features, though, represents a new style or a departure from Maugham's development as a writer of fiction.

But comedy in fiction was for Maugham a new style. Of the novels discussed in previous chapters—*Liza of Lambeth* (1897), *The Making of a Saint* (1898), *Mrs. Craddock* (1902), *Of Human Bondage* (1915), *The Moon and Sixpence* (1919)—all are characterized by the seriousness of their mood and tone. The one exception to this generalization is, of course, *The Making of a Saint:* there the reader is struck by the witty, humorous exchanges between Filippo and Matteo. Of course, Maugham developed and refined his skill in dialogue and comedy in his successful career as a playwright (1907–33). As Seymour Krim observes, playwriting taught him "economy of writing and pointed presentation," but most importantly "sure knowledge of his audience."[7] And a writer of comedy must certainly know his audience and have a clear idea of how they will react. The result in *Cakes and Ale* is what Mark Van Doren terms a "witty . . . satire."[8]

The comedy of *Cakes and Ale* is satiric in nature, not unlike that of *The Circle, Our Betters,* or *The Constant Wife.* But with the first-person dramatized narrator, Maugham is able to prepare the reader for subsequent dialogue. The resulting dramatic irony becomes an effective means of character portrayal. In fact, in this novel Maugham

exploits character portrayal—skillfully maintaining the gradual revelation of the personalities, consequences, motivations, values, and
goals of the characters—to such an extent that plot (which as a traditional storyteller Maugham always defended as being what readers
of fiction depended upon for interest and enjoyment) becomes less important than the character.

Another dimension of Maugham's technique in this work is the
novel's deceptive simplicity: the work is written in such a casual way
that it appears carelessly structured; the characters seem to meet as if
by mere chance, the style seems simple to the point of being sim-
plistic, the language seems common to the point of being clichélike,
and the characters are initially so plain and understandable that they
seem to be stereotypes. But as we examine Maugham's work more
closely we learn that this simplicity, ease, and naturalness are skillfully crafted.

An excellent example of the satiric and ironic manner in which
Maugham prepares the reader for subsequent dialogue is when Ashenden the narrator presents the distinctive qualities of Alroy Kear's
character:

[No] one could show a more genuine cordiality to a fellow novelist whose
name was on everybody's lips, but no one could more genially turn a cold
shoulder on him when idleness, or someone else's success had cast a shade
on his notoriety. . . .

Roy was very modest about his first novel. . . . He sent it with a pleasant
letter to all the leading writers of the day, and in this he told each one how
greatly he admired his works, how much he had learned from his study of
them, and how ardently he aspired to follow, albeit at a humble distance,
the trail his correspondent had blazed. (*CA*, 3, 7–8).

. . . if he [Roy] ran across Smith [a fellow novelist who is less successful
than Roy] at some gathering like the private view of the Royal Academy no
one could be more cordial. He wrung his hand and told him how delighted
he was to see him. Smith rejoiced in the glow of this wonderful vitality and
it was damned decent of Roy to say he'd give his eyeteeth to have written
a book half as good as Smith's last. On the other hand, if Roy thought
Smith had not seen him, he looked the other way. . . . (*CA*, 14–15)

In this way Maugham prepares the reader for dialogue between Ashenden and Roy—in which Ashenden suspects that Roy's reason for
being cordial and hospitable is not selfless, and that he wants a favor.

As his sense of being used and manipulated increases, Ashenden becomes increasingly sarcastic. And largely because the reader has been
so well prepared he or she needs no further explanation to understand
the motivation for Ashenden's behavior. Then only after being ex-
posed to a lengthy exchange with Roy does Ashenden finally explain
to the reader: "I knew I was irritating him and it gave me a pleasant
sensation." At last Ashenden manages to manipulate Roy, first into
dropping his mask of cordiality and false tolerance, and then into
striking back:

"His [Driffield's] sales have increased steadily every year and last year was
the best he ever had. You can take my word for that, Mrs. Driffield showed
me his accounts last time I was down there. Driffield has come to stay all
right."
    "Who can tell?"
    "Well, you think you can," replied Roy acidly. (CA, 32)

Finally Roy is silenced: "He looked in the bottom of his cup, but
whether to see if there were any more coffee in it or to find something
to say, I did not know" (CA, 34).

Later Ashenden begins to doubt his suspicion that Roy had a reason for inviting him. But as Roy accompanies Ashenden part of the
way home the conversation returns to the Driffields and to Rosie:

    "I suppose she was awful."
    "I don't recollect that."
    "She must have been dreadfully common. She was a barmaid wasn't she?"
    "Yes."
    "I wonder why the devil he married her. I've been given to understand
that she was extremely unfaithful to him."
    "Extremely."
    "Do you remember at all what she was like?"
    "Yes, very distinctly," I smiled. "She was sweet." (CA, 37)

It is around this subject that much of the incongruity of the work
centers. On the one hand, Roy and Amy Driffield place a high value
upon appearances and are willing to misrepresent the truth in order
to give the biography a sense of harmony. Their chief concern is to
support the position that Rosie was a damaging influence on Driffield: she did nothing to help his career and was "extremely unfaithful" to him. They also want to justify their belief that a "faithful"

portrait of Driffield was one that pointed to the positive influence
that Mrs. Trafford and Amy had had on his career. Even the elder
Driffield participates in this "unfaithful" world of appearances—although he is aware and in subtle ways lets Ashenden and the reader
see through his pretenses. On the other hand, Ashenden the narrator
defines for the reader what is "faithful" and "unfaithful." Ironically,
it is Rosie and the early Driffield who are "faithful," truthful, and
genuine, who place that which is genuine above appearances, and are
quite naturally more tolerant of others. Mrs. Hudson, Ashenden's
former landlady, represents a parallel to Rosie in her genuineness and
lack of affectation.

Ashenden urges Roy to present a faithful portrait of Driffield, to
portray him as not only a talented writer but also as a real person, a
person who at the end of a meal was in the habit of wiping his plate
clean with a piece of bread, who liked to sneak off to the Bear and
Key for a few beers, who for the last three years of his life never took
a bath:

> "Don't you think it would be more interesting if you went the whole hog
> and drew him warts and all?"
> "Oh, I couldn't. Amy Driffield would never speak to me again. She only
> asked me to do the life because she felt she could trust my discretion. I must
> behave like a gentleman and a writer."
> "It's very hard to be a gentleman and a writer.'
> "I don't see why. And besides, you know what critics are. If you tell the
> truth they only say you're cynical and it does an author no good to get a
> reputation for cynicism."

But Roy has the most trouble dealing with Rosie's part in Driffield's
life:

> "But how the devil am I to get over the first Driffield?"
> "The skeleton in the cupboard," I murmured.
> "She is damned awkward to deal with. . . . Amy has very decided views
> on the subject, but I don't see how I can possibly meet them."

He is aware of enough of the truth about Rosie's role in Driffield's
life to realize that the facts will be difficult to distort. He knows, in
spite of Amy's insistence, that "the fact remains that all of Driffield's
greatest books were written when he was living with Rosie" (*CA*,
156–59).

And of course the closer the reader comes to the truth about Rosie and Driffield, the greater the discrepancy between that knowledge and the understanding Roy and Amy have. They choose to persist in their judgment despite Ashenden's ironic insistence that they are wrong: " 'That's where you make a mistake,' I replied. 'She was a very nice woman. I never saw her in a bad temper. You only had to say you wanted something for her to give it to you. I never heard her say a disagreeable thing about anyone. She had a heart of gold' " (*CA*, 283). So, contrary to the notions of the Roy Kears and Amy Driffields, the reader knows—with Ashenden—that Rosie may be the one person in the novel who is genuine and true. It is, in fact, Roy and Amy who are insincere, hypocritical, false, and deceptive. As in Maugham's stage comedies, "form" becomes "deceit." The genuine, however unfaithful, is preferred to the staid, the conventional, the hypocritical.

Compensation and Sources

Cakes and Ale has an authenticity and a credibility—qualities for which many of Maugham's works have been praised, especially *Of Human Bondage*—that result largely from Maugham's carrying out his pattern of compensation. In this novel he follows his aesthetic credo of simplicity, lucidity, and euphony—an important dimension in this pattern of compensation: the qualities of communication that as a stammerer he was denied in speaking. But beyond this, Maugham developed the first-person dramatized narrator into a character who is a compensation for all that his speech impediment, his sense of inferiority, his aloofness and passivity denied him in his life. The narrator is a participant in the action, an individual sought out by others for his knowledge and sympathetic understanding. And yet the narrator is an individual with a critical and often cynical view of life, a good conversationalist, someone in whom others confide. As Calder has observed, "The *persona* is a manifestation of Maugham's search for emotional and physical liberty. . . ."[9] In short, Willie Ashenden, the narrator of *Cakes and Ale,* is all that Maugham wished to be but never could fully become.

Second, the authenticity and credibility of the novel results largely from Maugham's combining the two major sources of the material of his fiction: observed reality—the material with which he filled his notebooks, the goal he describes as developing the "sensitivity of a photographic plate"—and experienced reality. The novel was suggested to him, according to Morgan, by the pomp of Hardy's funeral in 1928.[10] There can be little doubt that much of Driffield is suggested by—if not modeled after—Thomas Hardy, including the second wife's part in the writing of his biography.[11] And although initially denying the connection, Maugham later, in the preface to the 1956 Modern Library edition of the work, written after Hugh Walpole's death, admitted that Walpole was the model for Kear. In fact, the controversy surrounding this aspect of the novel and Maugham's liberal use of live models were the bases for a thinly disguised attack upon Maugham in a novel called *Gin and Bitters* by A. Riposte or Elinor Mordaunt (pseudonym for Evelyn May Wiehe).[12]

But in *Cakes and Ale,* Maugham combines both sources: what he had observed and what he had experienced. By grounding the work in his personal experience, he is able to involve the reader more directly in the subject matter of the novel—as he had done in *Of Human Bondage.* Tapping again into the rich experience with Sue Jones, both traumatic and exciting, Maugham creates relationships and emotions comparable in intensity to those in *Of Human Bondage.* Writing now with the distance of over fifteen years since his rejection by Sue Jones in 1913, Maugham is able to bring his Willie Ashenden into an active and credible relationship with Rosie. And with his divorce from Syrie now completed and with his developing relationship with Gerald Haxton (who, like the narrator/persona, was adept socially in ways that he never could be), Maugham drew upon the strong and positive emotions of his past and present life. It is little wonder, then, that *Cakes and Ale* was always Maugham's favorite of his novels.

Dialogue and Nonverbal Communication

Much of the authenticity of *Cakes and Ale* results also from Maugham's ability to capture setting, atmosphere, and character through dialogue and approximations of dialogue, and through nonverbal communication. As Calder observes, "The most striking quality of *Cakes and Ale* is the range of settings and periods which it encompasses. It incorporates Victorian provincial life, Edwardian social and literary manners, and the Georgian scene two decades later."[13]

A typical example of the capacity of Maugham's dialogue to capture the uniqueness of characters and their relationship to one another

is the following in which the Ashenden character is talking with Lionel Hillier about his puzzlement over how Rosie has turned from the
"fresh pleasant-looking young woman" in Blackstable to the "lovely
creature whose beauty now practically everyone acknowledged":

> "I can explain that to you in half a jiffy," said Lionel Hillier. "She was
> only a fresh, buxom wench when I first met her. I made her beauty."
> I forget what my answer was, but I know it was ribald.
> "All right. That just shows you don't know anything about beauty. No
> one ever thought very much of Rosie till I saw her like the sun shining sil-
> ver. It wasn't till I painted it that anyone knew that her hair was the most
> lovely thing in the world."
> "Did you make her neck and her breasts and her carriage and her bones?"
> I asked.
> "Yes, damn you, that's just what I did do." (CA, 208–9)

In the following Mrs. Hudson betrays her own character in what is
essentially a dramatic monologue. The dialogue that follows then reveals Ashenden's reaction to her as well as his own feelings and
values:

> "Don't talk to me about the country. The doctor said I was to go there
> for six weeks last summer. It nearly killed me, I give you my word. The
> noise of it. All them birds singin' all the time, and the cocks crowin' and
> the cows mooin'. I couldn't stick it out. When you've lived all the years I
> 'ave in peace and quietness you can't get used to all that racket goin' on all
> the time."
> "Is there anything you want, Mrs. Hudson?" I asked.
> She fixed her beady eyes on me reflectively.
> "I don't know as there is, now you come to speak of it, except me 'ealth
> and strength for another twenty years so I can go on workin'." I do not
> think I am a sentimentalist, but her reply, unexpected but so characteristic,
> made a sudden lump come to my throat. (CA, 171)

But Maugham also employs the approximation of voices and dialogue
to give greater credibility to his characters and their settings—a technique used effectively in *Of Human Bondage*. In the following example
Maugham captures not only the typical routine of Mrs. Hudson but
also her genuineness, wholesomeness, and naturalness.

> Every morning she was up betimes to get the fire lit. . . . "My word it's
> bitter this morning"; and if she didn't hear you having your bath, a flat tin

bath that slipped under the bed, the water put in the night before to take the chill off, she'd say: "There now, there's my dining-room floor not up yet, 'e 'll be late for his lecture again" and she would come tripping upstairs and thump on the door and you would hear her shrill voice: "If you don't get up at once you won't 'ave time to 'ave breakfast, an' I've got a lovely 'addick for you." She worked all day long and she sang at her work and she was gay and happy and smiling. (*CA*, 166)

Beyond these dramatic accomplishments, though, Maugham makes use of nonverbal communication—such as gestures, smiles, facial expressions—to reveal character and to heighten the comic contrast between appearance and reality that is central to the theme of the work. Ashenden frequently refers to Driffield's smiles and facial expressions. And by so doing he offers the reader a key to the real individual beneath the public figure. In this way, of course, Ashenden makes the reader aware of the falsity of the manners and fashions of this literary scene in which Driffield is immersed. The winks, looks, and gazes that the elder Driffield gives Ashenden enable him and the reader to understand that despite the change from the jolly and vulgar Driffield in Blackstable to the aloof and masked figure in London, the early Driffield is still alive and aware of the falsity.

In an enlightening study of nonverbal communication, Katherine Fell argues convincingly that nonverbal clues function in a subtle but vital way to develop the theme that literary fame forces a writer to repress his creativity. The initial impression Ashenden has of Driffield is based almost completely upon nonverbal clues: beard, clothes, and smile. And while the early Driffield's smile signifies kind-heartedness and a certain mischievousness, the later Driffield's forced and stiff smile reveals a "repressed, cynical character." Another example of a nonverbal clue to Driffield's repressed self is in the scene in which Ashenden visits the elder Driffield. At first, Driffield acts as though he does not know him. Then, without any warning, Driffield suddenly winks at him. Fell comments: "The wink is so out of place on the 'distinguished old face' that Ashenden can hardly believe that it appeared at all. Immediately after the wink, Driffield's face becomes again 'composed, intelligently benign, and quietly observant.' "[14] While these nonverbal clues unmask the latter Driffield, there are also nonverbal signals of his being masked. His present shabby alpaca with grey trousers contrasts with his earlier bright knickerbocker suit and tight britches and luncheon suit of blue serge. Whereas earlier

he wore a beard (Ashenden remembers Driffield tugging at it when
they last saw him off at the train station), in London he either has
only a mustache or is clean shaven. Driffield's later loss of beard represents for Ashenden, who put Vaseline on his upper lip to make a
mustache grow, a loss of strength and manhood.

Dramatized Narrator

Having developed the dramatized first-person narrator in his earlier
fiction—*The Making of a Saint* (1898), *The Moon and Sixpence* (1919),
and *Ashenden* (1927)—Maugham introduces in *Cakes and Ale* a refined
Willie Ashenden, a fully participating character in the action of the
novel and a narrator who looks back over past years and guides the
reader through the past to the present. Clearly this is the most fully
developed dramatized narrator in Maugham's fiction.

Maugham skillfully develops the three dimensions of Ashenden:
Ashenden the narrator, the Maugham-like Ashenden, Ashenden the
character. In fact, this introduction of the Ashenden narrator provides
an individual with whom the reader can relate, a seemingly trustworthy individual with common, practical sense. "I have noticed that
when someone asks for you on the telephone and, finding you out,
leaves a message begging you to call him up the moment you come
in, and it's important, the matter is more often important to him
than to you. When it comes to making you a present or doing you
a favour most people are able to hold their impatience within reasonable bounds" (*CA*, 1). The reader is further impressed with the narrator's ability to bring the characters of the novel to life. Of Mrs.
Barton Trafford, a prominent devotee to the arts whose praise and
patronage helps Driffield become famous, the narrator says:

She was said to have been unhappily married in early life, but now for many
years has been congenially united to Barton Trafford, a clerk in the Home
Office and a well-known authority on prehistoric man. She gave you the curious impression of having no bones in her body and you felt that if you
pinched her skin (which of course my respect for her sex as well as something of quiet dignity in her appearance would have never allowed me to
do) your fingers would meet. When you took her hand it was more like
taking a filet of sole. Her face, notwithstanding its large features, had something fluid about it. When she sat it was as though she had no backbone
and were stuffed, like an expensive cushion, with swansdown. (*CA*, 187–
88).

The Ashenden narrator further wins the reader's trust in his ironic depiction of Alroy Kear. Of him, he says, "I could think of no one among my contemporaries who had achieved so considerable a position on so little talent" (*CA*, 18). And while pretending to be fair to Kear, Ashenden lets the reader know what he is really like: "Roy has never lost the modesty which in his youth was his most engaging trait." Then Ashenden allows Roy to speak for himself, thereby demonstrating the true nature of his character: "I used to think that one day I should write a really great novel, but I've long ceased even to hope for that . . . I think I can tell a good story and can create characters that ring true. And after all the proof of the pudding is in the eating: *The Eye of the Needle* sold thirty five thousand in England and eighty thousand in America, and for the serial rights of my next book I've got the biggest terms I've ever had yet" (*CA*, 10). And when the Ashenden character is invited to dine with Kear, he is suspicious of Roy's reasons for inviting him: "I could not bring myself to believe that at the height of the London season Alroy Kear would waste an hour on a fellow writer who was not a reviewer and had no influence in any quarter whatever in order to talk of Matisse, the Russian Ballet and Marcel Proust" (*CA*, 27). Soon, of course, he learns that Roy needs help dealing with Rosie, "the skeleton in the closet," in the biography he is writing of Driffield at the request of the second Mrs. Driffield. But the Ashenden narrator subsequently gives the reader an even clearer idea of Kear's true "modesty" when the Ashenden character suggests to Roy that he may well someday take Driffield's place as the Grand Old Man of English letters. Roy takes the bait and runs with it: "Barring accidents, by which I mean barring some genius who suddenly springs up and sweeps the board, I don't quite see how in another twenty or twenty-five years I can help having the field pretty well to myself" (*CA*, 146).

The Ashenden narrator also reveals to the reader the very qualities of trustworthiness and friendliness that have led other characters of the novel to confide in and trust the Ashenden character. In fact, the narrator allows the reader to see into the workings of his mind, drawing upon his memory for the substance of the narrative.

Though these recollections have taken so long to narrate they took but a little while to pass through my head. They came to me higgledy-piggledy, an incident and then a scrap of conversation that belong to a previous time, and I have set them down for the convenience of the reader and because I have a neat mind. One thing that surprised me was that even at that far distance I could remember distinctly what people looked like and even the gist of what they said, but only with vagueness of what they wore. (*CA*, 144–45)

I wish now that I had not started to write this book in the first person singular. It is all very well when you can show yourself in an amiable or touching light . . . but it is not so nice when you have to exhibit yourself as a plain damned fool. (*CA*, 215)

The intimacy that the narrator permits the reader here is distinctly more intense than previous Maughamian narrators have allowed. And here Maugham grants the reader a glimpse over his shoulder as he writes, a look into the very act of composing, into the process by which he invents his fictional world. At these times the Ashenden narrator moves closer to the writer—becoming Maugham-like Ashenden.

But at other times the narrator moves the other direction, toward the Ashenden character who is deeply involved in the action of the novel. Visiting his former landlady and asking her if there is anything she wants; and when she replies that there is nothing except " 'ealth and strength for another twenty years so I can go on workin'," Ashenden tells the reader: "I do not think I am a sentimentalist, but her reply, unexpected but so characteristic, made a sudden lump come in my throat" (*CA*, 171). He sees Rosie in London: "I noticed now, for the first time, that she was pretty. Her eyes were bluer than I remembered and her skin was like ivory" (*CA*, 177). More and more he falls for Rosie's beauty: "She looked . . . without answering, but her full red lips broke into their childlike, mischievous smile" (*CA*, 198–99); her eyes had the blue of cornflowers, and her smile was the gayest, the most friendly, the sweetest thing I ever saw" (*CA*, 202–3). He reacts to her beauty: "I stared at her and I stared at the picture [of Rosie] I had such a funny little feeling in my heart. It was as though someone softly plunged a sharp knife into it, but it was not an unpleasant sensation at all, painful but strangely agreeable; and then suddenly I felt quite weak at the knees" (*CA*, 202). Finally, the Ashenden character returns with Rosie one evening to his room after going to the theater. Without warning he suddenly breaks down: "A sob broke from my tight throat. . . . I was shy and lonely . . . (. . . lonely in the spirit) . . . I began to cry. . . . She stroked my smooth face. She rocked me back and forth as though I were a child in her arms. I kissed her breasts and I kissed her . . ." (*CA*, 217).

The reader never loses sight of Ashenden's range from Maugham-like individual, to trusted narrator, to involved character. And even though involved in the Ashenden narrator and the Ashenden character, the reader is often reminded that Maugham is allowing an intimacy with himself: the Maugham who grew up in Whitstable and lived his early life in London, who privately wrote himself out of a medical career into a literary career: "It was my introduction into the world of art and letters; I kept it a profound secret that in the privacy of my lodgings I was busily writing; I was excited to meet people who were writing also and I listened entranced to their conversation" (*CA*, 181).

But as trustworthy as the Ashenden narrator may seem, he is not completely reliable. We hear the narrator's voice speaking to us in the present about what happened many years ago. We must depend upon his memory. Also, we cannot completely separate the Ashenden narrator from the Ashenden character, whom we see at various times from his teenage years to near sixty years old. Furthermore, the narrator leaves us before the novel is completed, leaving us with the Ashenden character in the scene of his final awareness with the surprisingly youthful, elderly Rosie, now well over seventy years old.

Second, as the reader learns how deceptive one point of view can be, he or she realizes that this is exactly how all the information of the novel is being received: one point of view, that of the Ashenden narrator. An important thematic thread of the novel, in fact, concerns the deceptiveness of the limited knowledge that comes from one or too few points of view. There are, of course, many examples of this: Driffield not knowing at first of Rosie's unfaithfulness, the lack of understanding that Roy and Mrs. Driffield have of Rosie, and the Ashenden character being unaware for some time of Rosie's unfaithfulness to him. And as the reader begins to grasp the great injustice to Driffield and Rosie that will be done in the forthcoming biography by Alroy Kear, he or she suddenly is made aware of how little he or she understands Rosie. Because of the information the reader receives from the Ashenden narrator and the Ashenden character, he or she understands much more of the true Rosie than does Roy or Amy Driffield. But it is only at the end of the novel that the reader learns how little he or she understands of the motivations for Rosie's behav-

ior. For it is there that we learn of the death of Rosie's daughter, her
unfaithfulness on the night of grief following that loss, and much of
the dynamics of Rosie and Edward's relationship following that tragedy. Furthermore, Rosie never even knew that Driffield was aware of
her unfaithfulness to him that night until she, years later, read his
novel describing everything that happened. Therefore, like the reader
of Brontë's *Wuthering Heights* who gradually becomes aware of the un-
reliable nature of the Nelly Dean narrator, so the reader of *Cakes and
Ale* gradually becomes aware that the Ashenden narrator is not as
trustworthy as he at first seemed. Like Maugham himself, the Ashenden narrator does not have all the answers to life's ironies and tragedies, has little control over the direction that life takes. When
Willie confronts Rosie with her unfaithfulness to him, she replies:

> "Oh, my dear, why d'you bother your head about any others? What harm
> does it do you? Don't I give you a good time? Aren't you happy when you're
> with me?"
> "Awfully."
> "Well, then. It's so silly to be fussy and jealous. Why not be happy with
> what you can get? Enjoy yourself while you have the chance, I say; we shall
> all be dead in a hundred years and what will anything matter then? Let's
> have a good time while we can." She put her arms round my neck and
> pressed her lips against mine. I forgot my wrath. I only thought of her
> beauty and her enveloping kindness.
> "You must take me as I am, you know," she whispered.
> "All right," I said. (*CA*, 230–31)

In a similar way, life must be accepted on its own terms, taken as it
is. Rosie is what she is largely because of her nature, her personality—warm, generous, personable, kind. And her life has worked out
the way it has largely because of circumstances and situations that
have developed, mostly beyond her control. Her meeting Edward,
her pregnancy, their marriage, the death of their child, their moving
from Blackstable to London because of debts and his career, meeting
Willie and the others, even George Kemp coming to her for sympathy that night—all these are events and circumstances that are mainly
not of her choosing. And unlike most of the other characters in the
novel, she is true and faithful to her nature and circumstances.

But this awareness also comes gradually to the reader through the
interplay of the narrator and character. We begin with the Ashenden
narrator in the present and the Ashenden character in the present.

Then through flashbacks we move from the present to the past, where we see the Ashenden character as a youngster. Through a series of these back-and-forth movements we come toward the present. But before the novel ends the Ashenden narrator departs, leaving us with the Ashenden character in the final scene with Rosie.

More important, though, than these structural devices is Maugham's depiction of the growth of the Ashenden character. At first he is shocked at the unconventional behavior of Edward and Rosie—not attending church, associating indiscriminately with seemingly everyone, Rosie's having been a barmaid. Later he is disturbed at their running away from Blackstable without paying their debts; later their being friendly toward him in London; Rosie's being unfaithful to Edward, and then to him. Finally, he is shocked that she left Edward and ran away with George Kemp, an act that is for him then inexcusable and unbelievable. As before, though, the Ashenden character has greater and greater difficulty condemning Rosie for her behavior. In fact, he becomes progressively more tolerant.

When Kuyper, one of Rosie's lovers, left town he presented her with a fur coat. Ashenden, having refused to admit Rosie's unfaithfulness, is forced to face the truth: Rosie is able to afford such comforts as a beautiful cape because she shares her bed with generous men: "And then I knew that the suspicion that I refused to believe was true; I knew that when she went out to dinner with Quentin Forde and Harry Retford and Lionel Hillier she went to bed with them just as she came to bed with me" (*CA*, 228). Here, of course, we have the mature voice of the *narrator* giving us his perception of the past and his growing awareness of the *character*. And throughout the novel we have the presence of this more mature Ashenden to guide us. Toward the end of the Ashenden character's time with Roy Kear and Amy Driffield in Blackstable, he asks Amy when Rosie died:

"Oh, about ten years ago."
"How did you hear?" I asked.
"From Harold Kemp, the son . . . I never told Edward." (*CA*, 287)

At this point the narrator, providing more information, tells us the truth: "I chuckled when I reflected what a bombshell I could throw if I chose. There was one person who could tell them all they wanted to know about Edward Driffield and his first marriage; but this fact

I proposed to keep to myself. They thought Rosie was dead, they erred. Rosie was very much alive" (*CA*, 288–89)

And as much as we come to depend upon the narrator, we gradually become aware that he does not know the whole truth. Of course, as the Ashenden character matures we have less need of the narrator. But just before the Ashenden narrator departs for the remaining lines of the novel, he moves toward the Maugham-like Ashenden, to comment on the writer being the only free person because he can rid himself of unpleasantness, "unrequited love, wounded pride, anger at the treachery of someone to whom he has shown kindness. . . ." Here, of course, we again come close to Somerset Maugham who once more—as in *Of Human Bondage*—is grounding his work in his own emotional experiences, writing now of past loves and sorrows with considerable distance:

I began to meditate upon the writer's life. It is full of tribulation. First he must endure poverty and the world's indifferences; then, having achieved a measure of success, he must submit with a good grace to its hazards. He depends upon a fickle public. He is at the mercy of journalists. . . . But he has one compensation. Whenever he has anything on his mind, whether it be a harassing reflection, grief at the death of a friend, unrequited love, wounded pride, anger at the treachery of someone to whom he has shown kindness, in short any emotion or any perplexing thought, he has only to put it down in black and white, using it as a theme of a story, or the decorating of an essay, to forget all about it. He is the only free man. (*CA*, 305–6)

Then we as readers are left alone with the Ashenden character, perhaps near the age of the author when he was writing this novel—mid-fifties—and Rosie, now over seventy. We and the character have questions that we want answered: "why did Rosie go away with George Kemp" (of whom we have a rather unfavorable view)? But beyond this we and the Ashenden character wonder: "what did she ever see in him?" Here we discover the truth about Rosie and her *faithfulness;* faithful to herself, the cards that life has dealt her she has played as she could—no better, no worse. Lord George Kemp came to Rosie that night and " 'said that everything had gone wrong and he was hurt and there'd be a warrant out for his arrest in a few days and he was going to America and would I go with him as well, what could I do? I couldn't let him go all that way by himself. . . .' 'I wonder what it was you saw in him.' . . . 'I'll tell you,' said Rosie.

'He was always such a perfect gentleman' " (*CA,* 307–8). It is here at the end of the novel that the three voices, the three Ashendens (the Ashenden-character, the Ashenden-narrator, and the Maugham-like Ashenden) come together and we as readers are no longer working our way toward the present; we are there with Willie and Rosie.

In fact, we have not only reached the beginning point, the present where the Ashenden narrator began, but with the Ashenden character we move toward the future—leaving Roy and Amy far behind with their struggles to do away with the skeleton in the cupboard.

Chapter Eight
Conclusion

In a 1927 letter to Paul Dottin, Maugham outlined the writing that he projected for the next ten years and stated that he would end with a work summing up his opinions and works. He obviously projected this work as a final rounding off of his life, a completion of the pattern that he had designed for himself.

In 1938 Maugham published *The Summing Up,* an autobiographical work. Although he lived for another twenty-seven years and continued to write and publish, Maugham was correct in the projection that his major work would be completed by this date. He had written his last play, *Sheppey,* in 1933 and his last travel book, *Don Fernando,* in 1935. He published four collections of short stories (in 1931, 1936, 1940, 1947), three collections of essays (in 1948, 1952, 1956), two reminiscences (both in 1962), and his notebook (1949). And Maugham did publish six novels (in 1939, 1941, 1942, 1944, 1946, 1948), of which *The Razor's Edge* (1944) is the most important. But, as he predicted, his pattern was for the most part completed with the publication of *The Summing Up* in 1938.

Justifying A Life

In one sense, *The Summing Up* is not an autobiography; it is not a work that takes up the whole life in a complete and chronological manner. But there is a sense in which it is an apologia: autobiographical writing justifying and defending the life that the author has lived. There is also a sense in which this work is a "confession," a confession of what Maugham believed and lived by, as well as an account of the strong and weak points of his life. He knew these literary traditions well. But there is yet a more important sense in which *The Summing Up* in its concealment and revelation pattern and in its embarrassingly frank manner of presenting his shortcomings captures the essence of Maugham's personality.

Warning that the work is "not an autobiography" because "no one can tell the whole truth" (*SU,* 10), Maugham announces his intention to conceal much of his life from the reader: "I have no desire to lay bare my heart, and I put limits to the intimacy that I wish the reader to enter upon with me. There are matters on which I am content to maintain my privacy" (*SU,* 10). But the reader soon realizes that much of what he says here is more of a pose than the real stance that Maugham will take—especially as he reveals so much of what is of value to him: in belief, philosophy, principles in writing, audiences, writing styles, etc. Always, though, one senses that Maugham is concealing a degree of truth, demanding his privacy. It is in this way, then, that *The Summing Up* fits the general pattern that Maugham has well established in his work—a pattern of concealment and revelation.

And the *manner* in which these insights are presented is as important in capturing the essential personality of Maugham as *what* is revealed. For example, the reader is caught up short when Maugham reveals intimate emotions and attitudes about himself. He speaks of his sense of being limited as a writer and person, of having little imagination, of having only a partial self to portray, of not experiencing the emotions of common men—and therefore never reaching the level of the great writers, that he has a logical brain but not a very powerful one, etc. Many of these statements are questionable: for instance, Maugham has an imagination that was certainly adequate for all of his inventions; he does not lack imagination—in the true sense of the word. In fact, greater use of metaphoric language with the plain style he had chosen would not only be inappropriate but would result in an ineffective style, one that did not fit the subject matter.

Beyond the questionable truthfulness of these statements the reader is curious about Maugham's purpose in making them. In this regard, one is struck by the similar extreme behavior of his fictional characters, stepping beyond what seem reasonable bounds to bring suffering on themselves. Philip deliberately inflicts pain on himself by financing Mildred in her unfaithfulness to him when going away with his friend Griffiths. Cordell terms this behavior "masochistic . . . a morbid desire to be tortured," and points to this behavior as a "need for suffering."[1] Similarly, Dick Stroeve in *The Moon and Sixpence* moves out of his studio to allow Blanche, his wife, to carry on a love affair there with the artist Charles Strickland. Stroeve even divides their possessions, giving her half of all they own. Interesting in light of these fictional portrayals of emotion is Cordell's statement that these extremes were grounded in Maugham's experiences: seized by a "devil of self torture," he actually gave "his rival five pounds."[2]

There is then considerable evidence of the influence of Maugham's deep-seated sense of inferiority, often exhibited in compensatory behavior, attitudes, and drives, as well as self-deprecation—as in the above statements.[3] Of course, this pattern is not unlike that of the Maughamian persona/narrator. In *The Summing Up* these statements may strike the reader as inappropriate and not adding to the purpose of this autobiographical work. But considered as an actual autobiography, one can see how well it captures the essential Maugham and picks up a major thread in Maugham's highly individual pattern.

In the work Maugham allows the reader to understand much of the way he wrote, what he believed about life and his works, and his ideas on other writers. He underscores the fact that he drew heavily from his own life experiences: "In one way or another I have used in my writings whatever has happened to me in the course of my life . . . but fact and fiction are . . . intermingled" (*SU*, 1).

As mentioned earlier, modern readers are fascinated with the way in which Maughamian persona/narrators are drawn to, puzzled by extremes in individuals—particularly the genius, artist, saint—but, like most readers, they are thrown back to the real, the practical world: "The ordinary is the writer's richer field" (*SU*, 6). But the pattern of puzzlement followed by revelation is central to Maugham's work.

There is no more merit in having read a thousand books than in having ploughed a thousand fields. There is no more merit in being able to attach a correct description to a picture than in being able to find out what is wrong with a stalled motor-car. . . . The artist has no excuse when he uses others with condescension. He is a fool if he thinks his knowledge is more important than theirs and an oaf if he cannot comfortably meet them on equal footing. (*SU*, 86)

And that, of course, is what Maugham achieved: never condescending to his readers, meeting them on equal footing.

But it was more than an attitude that endeared Maugham to the common reader; his practical, down-to-earth views had their influence: "money was like the sixth sense without which you could not make the most of the other five" (*SU*, 112); "love was only the dirty trick nature played on us to achieve the continuation of the species"

(*SU*, 71); "I would much sooner spend a month on a desert island with a veterinary surgeon than with a prime minister" (*SU*, 6); "I have wished that beside his bunch of flowers at the Old Bailey, his lordship had a packet of toilet paper" (*SU*, 55); "I knew that suffering did not ennoble, it degraded" (*SU*, 62).

The writing of *The Summing Up* was a significant act for Maugham. As illustrated in his 1927 letter, it was a work that he planned many years before completing it. It was obviously a pattern of Maugham's to impose on life a form with a beginning, a middle, and an end. The work was simply necessary in the pattern. He had to write it: "i have written because I had a fertile invention [hardly any admission of lack of imagination here] and the ideas for plays and stories that thronged my brain would not let me rest till I had rid of them by writing them."[4] Over and over he repeats this belief of the cathartic nature of writing.[5] But also in writing the work Maugham put his life and work into a form that gave him distance and a perspective on himself that few individuals ever have.

Puzzlement in Fiction

Factors beyond the text—such as Maugham's celebrity status, image as a British gentleman, secret agent during World War I, tasteful craftsman of fiction, and a model of the effective use of the queen's English—undoubtedly influenced the reception of each of his later works. In *The Razor's Edge,* Maugham's pattern continues. He approaches the readers as equals—respected members of the audience and as fellow travelers on adventures of life, one in whom he confides. He begins: "I have never begun a novel with more misgiving. If I call it a novel it is only because I don't know what else to call it." Thus, his growing number of readers knew immediately that they had yet another treat ahead of them.

In *The Razor's Edge,* the last novel in the tradition of *The Moon and Sixpence* and *Cakes and Ale,* the Ashenden narrator/character is named Mr. Maugham. Visiting in Chicago, he is contacted by a friend of many years, Mr. Elliott Templeton (a close parallel to Alroy Kear), and invited to dinner. That evening Maugham meets Isabel, Elliott's niece, Isabel's mother, Gray (who will eventually marry Isabel despite her preference for Larry), Sophie, a friend of the family, and most noteworthy, Larry Darrell, Isabel's fiancé, who has just returned from the war. With Elliott, Mr. Maugham will have a relationship very much like that between Mr. Ashenden and Alroy Kear. Larry is the

character about whom Mr. Maugham has a sense of puzzlement—
similar to that between Willie Ashenden and Rosie and between the
narrator and Charles Strickland. And the relationship between Isabel
and Mr. Maugham is warm and open, yet flirtatious at times and at
others quite critical. This relationship Mr. Maugham no doubt had
with a few women in his life—perhaps most notably with Barbara
Back, wife of Ivor Back, the prominent London surgeon, and with
the novelist G. B. Stern.

Mr. Maugham is at first impressed and later quite puzzled by
Larry. Then he learns that Larry has put off his marriage to Isabel,
feeling that he must go to Paris and to the East in search of the
meaning and purpose of life—to find God. Still later he learns that
Larry had a friend in the war who lost his life saving Larry from certain death. This and his natural goodness and sensitive nature lead
Larry on a quest for meaning and answers.

Maugham cultivates the special relationship that he has established
with his readers. He takes unusual liberties in developing this highly
structured work—which on the surface may seem quite casual (moving back and forth in time, using the flashback technique, a narrator
who is a world traveler)—all a plausible harmony. In a sense the
reader is a fellow traveler with Maugham.

Typical of the personas of earlier works, the Mr. Maugham narrator shows a fascination with an exceptional individual such as Larry
gradually becomes. Although modern readers no doubt identify with
Mr. Maugham's attraction to such a saintly individual, they most
likely relate even more strongly to Mr. Maugham's inability to reach
the same lofty heights as Larry does. These dimensions of the novel
and of reader participation were present in other novels, of course—
notably in *Cakes and Ale*. Here, though, readers experience the emotions and attitudes from a greater distance, have less of a sense of
what Larry's life and values meant than, for instance, Strickland's or
Driffield's. Mr. Maugham's answer to his lack of understanding
comes at the end of the novel: "I am of the earth, earthy; I can only
admire the radiance of such a rare creature, I cannot step into his
shoes and enter into his inmost heart as I sometimes think I can do
with persons more nearly allied to the common run of men."[5] In contrast to Larry, Mr. Maugham, the English gentleman, sees life
through the eyes of moderation, pragmatism, objectivity.

The novel follows the common Maughamian pattern of concealment: concealing information—about Larry's quest, his adventures,

his findings, etc.—and revelation: revealing the emotions and attitudes of the narrator, Isabel, Larry, Sophie, and Elliott. And there are close parallels here to *Cakes and Ale* and *The Moon and Sixpence:* Larry to Rosie and Strickland; Mr. Maugham to Willie Ashenden; Elliott Templeton to Alroy Kear, etc.

Mr. Maugham presents the novel in a deceptively casual manner—admitting misgivings for even calling it a novel, etc. But beneath this surface informality the reader finds a highly structured, intricately worked-out system of individuals, use of time, events, etc. We know of the date of the opening, reference is made to the publication of *The Moon and Sixpence,* ages are given of characters, dates of events—such as the stock market crash, etc.—that give the novel historic credibility.

But beyond this craftfulness there is a shift in concern from plot to character—as was true in *Cakes and Ale.* That is, the novel concerns Larry—about whom we learn very little. At the beginning of chapter 6, in the heart of the novel, Mr. Maugham states: "I feel it right to warn the reader that he can very well skip this chapter without losing the thread of the story as I have to tell, since for the most part it is nothing more than the account of a conversation that I had with Larry." He adds ironically that if it had not been for this conversation he would not have written the book. Here the Mr. Maugham narrator/author (as the two are fusing at this point) teases the reader, enticing him or her to read further. Also here Mr. Maugham is shifting the focus on character, that of Larry. As in countless other Maugham novels the involvement is an intensely dramatic one. And what the reader comes away with is, like the Persian rug, in direct proportion to what he or she has put into it; it is an experience in which there is no intrinsic meaning.

Legacy

What Richard Ellmann says concerning Joyce's life could be easily said about Maugham's: "the life of an artist . . . differs from the lives of other persons in that its events are becoming artistic sources even as they command his present attention. Instead of allowing each day, pushed back by the next, to lapse into imprecise memory, he shapes again the experiences which have shaped him. He is at once the captive and the liberator. . . . the process of reshaping experience becomes a part of his life, another of its recurrent events like rising or sleeping."[6]

Maugham gave artistic form to the experiences and emotions of his life in such a way that he involved his readers dramatically. Though un-English and unmodern in his emphasis upon form and stressing the importance of "the story," Maugham offered an appealing stance and attitude for the modern reader. He believed that a novelist should not preach or teach, but entertain. He considered himself devoid of the pedagogical instinct. Art should always seem a pleasant accident, he felt. Accordingly, his great achievement was to write simply, clearly, and naturally. Not a poetic novelist or an innovator—at least in the usual sense, for Maugham exploited his considerable dramatic skills in his plain style. The result, as has been observed, was a subtle, refined dramatic fiction, exhibited nowhere better than in *Cakes and Ale.*

The dramatized narrator of Maugham's fiction, as it touches on and gains strength from the psychological depths of his personality (inferiority, compensation, social interest, etc.), ultimately becomes one of the finest achievements in modern British literature. As Graham Greene has observed, Maugham will be remembered as "the narrator."[7] The dramatic intensity of his best work can "arouse our pity and deepen our tolerance and understanding; and, more subtly, he can raise in the reader's mind the misgiving that what is sometimes smugly regarded as tolerance may only be indifference."[8]

Maugham's legacy may well be the honest, unsentimental interest that he took in people and the skill with which he transformed experience into fiction. The courage of overcoming his limitations in speaking and other real and felt inferiorities gave him strength, and he never stopped writing to the very end of his long life. But the interest in others and his desire to write was present early in his career. For instance, in the *Academy* of 13 September 1897, Maugham replied to a reviewer who complained of the lack of hope and optimism in *Liza of Lambeth.*

Of course the story is sordid and nasty: it is meant to be. If the book was to be written at all it had to be done truthfully. . . .

I suppose no one can tell why the desire comes to him to write about a certain thing—but besides the feeling that I was writing because I could not help it, was another, that possibly it might induce the Philistine to look a little less self-righteously at the poor, and even to pity their unhappiness.

I am sorry that your reviewer should "quit me with a grimy feeling, as if he had had a mud bath in all the filth of a London street." But perhaps he will not entirely forget me; and next time he is forced to go through some slums, he will not push aside with his umbrella the ragged child who is in his way, and when he sees a woman with a black eye, her face all pale and tear-stained, he may not look upon her entirely with contempt.[9]

Maugham was of course quite young here. But he never lost the honesty and interest in others, never stopped urging his readers to be tolerant.

Even the anxiety that Maugham felt in the final years was a manifestation of his social interest, an assurance that he needed to know that his attempts to contribute to the literature of his country had been worthwhile, that he would continue to be read. His wish, as in his 1897 letter to the *Academy,* was that he not be "entirely forgotten."

The Last of "Willie"
(To Richard A. Cordell, Willie's Friend)

How painful those last dimly conscious years
      for Maugham to feel faintly
the world's scholars working,
some waiting till life was gone . . . and the market right.
      And for the first time
          his great strength failed;
    worse, his attention lost focus.

But in the calm, vaguely felt moments,
when he again became aware of their working,
a hinted smile of satisfaction would come
as he thought of the designed pattern
      for his work,
          his life,
              his world,
of the care he had taken, even with that considered weak.
      (Weak? *Strong?* What difference now?)
      Beginning.
          Middle.
            End.

Too soon, as a child's, his attention is caught away:
      Something beyond—a noise,
a bird in flight watched from a villa window?

Then, once more, "the English Maupassant,"
    "the craftsman" with his "mixture as before,"
        "the strange old man of fiction"—

    the artist . . .
is lost to the world.

And far, far away in the world's libraries,
    his works are being checked out. [10]

Notes and References

Chapter One

1. *The Summing Up* (London; 1938), 46; hereafter cited in the text as *SU*.
2. Frederic Raphael, *W. Somerset Maugham and His World* (New York; 1976), 7.
3. Frederic Maugham, *At the End of the Day* (Westport, Conn.: Heinemann, 1951), 15.
4. Ibid., 15.
5. Ibid., 11, 4–5.
6. Raphael, *W. Somerset Maugham,* 8.
7. F. Maugham, *At the End,* 15.
8. Ibid., 17.
9. Ibid., 15.
10. "Looking Back," *Show: A Magazine of the Arts,* June 1962, 63; hereafter cited in the text as *L*.
11. Raphael, *W. Somerset Maugham,* 9.
12. F. Maugham, *At the End,* 19.
13. Raphael, *W. Somerset Maugham,* 7–9.
14. F. Maugham, *At the End,* 20.
15. Raphael, *W. Somerset Maugham,* 10.
16. Ted Morgan, *Maugham* (New York, 1980), 14.
17. Ibid., 15.
18. Ibid., 16.
19. Anthony Curtis, *Somerset Maugham* (London, 1977), 24.
20. Lee Edward Travis, ed., *A Handbook of Speech Pathology and Audiology* (New York: Appleton-Century-Crofts, 1971), 1075.
21. "Some Novelists I have Known," in *The Vagrant Mood* (London, 1952), 232–42; hereafter cited in the text as *VM*.
22. Travis, ed., *Handbook,* 1013.
23. Morgan, *Maugham,* 160.
24. Curtis, *Somerset Maugham,* 29.
25. *Cakes and Ale* (New York, 1930), 79; hereafter cited in the text as *CA*.
26. Morgan, *Maugham,* 12.
27. Curtis, *Somerset Maugham,* 27.
28. Ibid., 30.
29. Raphael, *W. Somerset Maugham,* 10.
30. Curtis, *Somerset Maugham,* 32–33.

31. Ibid., 33.

32. F. Maugham, *At the End,* 15.

33. Curtis, *Somerset Maugham,* 35.

34. Cyril Connolly, *Enemies of Promise* (New York: Macmillan 1948), 30.

35. Curtis, *Somerset Maugham,* 38.

36. Ibid., 42–43.

37. Morgan, *Maugham,* 23.

38. Ibid., 23.

39. Ibid., 24–25.

40. Travis, ed., *Handbook,* 1018–19.

41. John Money and Patricia Tucker, *Sexual Signatures: On Being a Man or a Woman* (Boston: Little Brown, 1975), 59.

42. Morgan, *Maugham,* 38.

43. See William L. Lane, *The New International Commentary of the New Testament,* ed. F. F. Bruce (Grand Rapids: Eerdmans, 1974), esp. 513–19.

44. Brian Finny, *Christopher Isherwood: A Critical Biography* (New York: Oxford *University Press,* 1979), 180.

45. Noel Coward, Foreword to *Remembering Mr. Maugham,* by Garson Kanin (New York: Atheneum, 1966), vi.

46. Richard Ellmann, Introduction to *Oscar Wilde: A Collection of Essays* (Englewood Cliffs, N.J.: Prentice-Hall, 1969), 2.

47. Karl G. Pfeiffer, *W. Somerset Maugham: A Candid Portrait* (New York: W. W. Norton, 1959.)

48. Richard Heron Ward, *William Somerset Maugham* (London, 1937), 58.

49. Rollo May, *Love and Will* (New York: Dell, 1969), 21.

50. Morgan, *Maugham,* 32; quoting Joseph B. Lurie.

51. Henry F. Salerno, *English Drama in Transition, 1880–1920* (New York: Western, 1968), 23.

52. Morgan, *Maugham,* 31, 43.

53. Salerno, *English Drama,* 23.

54. Maugham donated this manuscript to the Library of Congress on the condition that it never be published.

55. "Augustus," in *The Vagrant Mood.*

56. *The Writer's Point of View* (London, 1951), 22; hereafter cited in the text as *WPV.*

57. Ellmann, "Foreword," xi.

58. Morgan, *Maugham,* 111.

59. Connolly, *Enemies,* 58.

60. Ibid., 66.

61. Morgan, *Maugham,* 181.

62. Ibid., 199, 221–22, 208.

63. Ibid., 190.

64. Ibid., 302.

65. Frank Swinnerton, *The Georgian Scene* (New York: Rinehart Farrar, 1939), 261.

66. Richard Aldington, "Somerset Maugham: An Appreciation," *Saturday Evening Review* 20 (19 August 1939):12.

67. Maugham's cottage in South Carolina was on the banks of a river, with a magnificent view of the marsh. It was built on Doubleday's thousand-acre plantation, hidden in rows of pines. The cottage was two miles from the Doubleday house, nineteen from a village, and fifty from a town. It was, in short, the ideal setting for a writer.

68. Morgan, *Maugham*, 180.

69. Martin S. Day, *History of English Literature* (New York: Doubleday, 1964), 3:432.

70. Morgan, *Maugham*, 4.

71. Gerald Kelly to Bertram Alanson, 3 March 1953, Stanford University.

72. Klaus Jonas, *The Maugham Enigma* (New York, 1959).

73. Morgan, *Maugham*, xiv, 206.

Chapter Two

1. Raymond Toole Stott, *A Bibliography of the Works of W. Somerset Maugham* (London, 1973), 229.

2. Maugham to Paul Dottin, 1927; Humanities Research Center, University of Texas at Austin.

3. Alfred Adler, *What Life Should Mean to You* (New York: Grosset & Dunlap, 1931), 19.

4. Alfred Adler, *Social Interest* (New York: Putnam & Sons, 1933), 212–13.

5. *Of Human Bondage* (London, 1936), 1; hereafter cited in the text as *OHB*.

6. Alfred Adler, *The Individual Psychology of Alfred Adler* (New York: Basic Books, 1956), 241–42.

7. Ibid., 830–31.

8. Robin Maugham, "My Uncle Willie," *Saturday Evening Post*, 29 Jan 1966, 80.

9. Adler, *Individual Psychology*, 381.

10. Ibid., 368.

11. Heinz L. Ansbacher, "The Concept of Social Interest," *Journal of Individual Psychology* 24 (1968):140.

12. Ibid., 145.

13. Ibid.

14. Adler, *Individual Psychology*, 133.

15. Ibid.

16. Ansbacher, "Concept of Social Interest," 147.

17. Robert Lorin Calder, *W. Somerset Maugham and the Quest for Freedom* (London, 1972), 212.

18. Charles Henry Hawtrey, *The Truth At Last* (Boston: Little Brown, 1924), vii.

19. Ibid., vi.

20. Gilbert Highet, *The Art of Teaching* (New York: Knopf, 1950), 110.

21. Richard Cordell Introduction to *Of Human Bondage* (New York: Random House, 1956), xi.

Chapter Three

1. Glenway Westcott, Foreword to *The Summing Up* (New York: Signet, 1964), xxii.

2. With the exception of propaganda writing during World II and a few introductions and forewords to the works of others, Maugham confined his efforts to literature.

3. John Russell Taylor, *The Rise and Fall of the Well-Made Play* (London: Methuen, 1967), 92.

4. It must be remembered that English drama in the nineteenth century was at a low ebb; whereas the novel was on the ascent.

5. Ward, *William Somerset Maugham,* 57.

6. Cordell, *William Somerset Maugham,* 134.

7. Raphael, *W. Somerset Maugham,* 21.

8. *A Writer's Notebook* (London, 1949), 38; hereafter cited in the text *WN.*

9. *Liza of Lambeth* (London: Heinemann, 1897), 2; hereafter cited in the text as *LOL.*

10. In the preface to the collected edition of *Cakes and Ale* Maugham speaks of his early admiration for Hardy, for *Tess of the D'Urbervilles,* and for Tess: "I read *Tess of the D'Urbervilles* when I was eighteen with such enthusiasm that I determined to marry a milkmaid . . ." (14).

11. Morgan, *Maugham,* 57.

12. Thomas Maitland (Robert Buchanan), "The Fleshly School of Poetry," *Contemporary Review,* October 1871.

13. In this, his most considerable poetic work, George Meredith, a popular poet and novelist in Maugham's youth, tells the story of the tragic dissolution of a marriage (founded upon his own marital experience) with such dramatic intensity that it has qualities of a novel. Critics attacked Meredith for his cynicism, for flippancy, and for making a great moral mistake in publishing the work.

14. Ward, *William Somerset Maugham,* 122.

15. Calder, *W. Somerset Maugham,* 46.

16. Ward, *William Somerset Maugham,* 122.

17. *Academy,* 13 September 1897.

18. Calder, *W. Somerset Maugham,* 47.

19. Raphael, *W. Somerset Maugham,* 21.

20. Calder, *W. Somerset Maugham,* 42.

21. Ibid., 40, 48, 50.

22. Ibid., 46–47, 50.

23. Curtis, *Somerset Maugham,* 4.

24. Raphael, *W. Somerset Maugham,* 21.

25. Calder, *W. Somerset Maugham,* 41.

26. *Academy,* 13 September 1897.

27. Ward, *William Somerset Maugham,* 58.

28. Walter Allen, *The English Novel* (London: Phoenix House, 1949), esp. 271, 287, 312–14.

29. Raphael, *W. Somerset Maugham,* 27.

30. Morgan, *Maugham,* 66.

31. Raymond Toole Stott, *A Bibliography of the Works of William Somerset Maugham* (London, 1973), 16–19.

32. But the year after Maugham's death, L. C. Page of Boston brought out an edition of the work.

33. *Spectator* (London) 71 (6 August 1898):184.

34. *Academy,* 1 July 1899, 15; 17 September 1898, 270.

35. *Dial* 25 (16 September 1898):172.

36. *Athenaeum,* no. 3690 (16 July 1898):95.

37. *Bookman* (London) 14 (September 1898):169.

38. *New York Evening Post Literary Review,* 15 July 1922, 81.

39. *Literature* 3 (27 August 1898):185–86.

40. *The Collected Plays of William Somerset Maugham* (London: Heinemann, 1952), xiv.

41. *The Making of a Saint* (London, 1898), 14; hereafter cited in the text as *MS.*

42. Woodburn O. Ross, "William Somerset Maugham: Theme and Variations," *College English* 8 (December 1946):113–22.

43. Calder, *W. Somerset Maugham,* 60.

44. Ibid.

45. Morgan, *Maugham,* 89.

46. Edwin Francis Edgett, "The Devious Ways of Somerset Maugham," *Boston Evening Transcript,* 16 June 1920, 6.

47. Raphael, *W. Somerset Maugham,* 29.

48. Calder, *W. Somerset Maugham,* 61.

49. Morgan, *Maugham,* 88–89.

50. Calder, *W. Somerset Maugham,* 60.

51. J. Dobrinsky, "Comptes Rendus," *Etudes Anglaises* 9 (July–September 1956):266–67.

52. A. S. John Adcock, *Bookman* (London) 23 (December 1902):108.

53. *Bookman* 67 (May 1928):xxi.

54. *Athenaeum,* no. 3924 (11 January 1903):44.

55. Dobrinsky, "Comptes Rendus," 266–67.

56. Matti Paavilainen, *Ylioppilaslehti,* 13 September 1957, 8.

57. Calder, *W. Somerset Maugham,* 152–53.

58. Raphael, *W. Somerset Maugham,* 29.

59. Morgan, *Maugham,* 90–91.

60. Stott, *Bibliography,* 29.

61. Morgan, *Maugham,* 90.

62. Raphael, *W. Somerset Maugham,* 29.

63. Calder, *W. Somerset Maugham,* 65.

64. Morgan, *Maugham,* 92–93.

Chapter Four

1. St. John Ervine, "Maugham: The Playwright," in *The World of Somerset Maugham,* ed. Klaus Jonas (New York: British Book Centre, 1959), 149.

2. Morgan, *Maugham,* 136–37.

3. Walter P. Eaton, "The Dramatist: A Playwright Who Stumbled Into Fame," in *The Maugham Enigma,* ed. Jonas (New York, 1954), 102.

4. *Lady Frederick* in *The Collected Plays,* 6 vols. (London, 1931–34), 1:28; hereafter cited in the text as *CP.*

5. Curtis, *Somerset Maugham,* 74.

6. Ward, *William Somerset Maugham,* 202.

7. *London Times,* 28 October 1907, 12.

8. *Graphic,* 2 November 1907, 610.

9. *Academy,* 2 November 1907, 97–97.

10. *New York Sun,* 10 November 1908, 7.

11. *Academy,* 4 January 1908, 324.

12. *New York Dramatic Mirror,* 21 November 1908, 2.

13. Eaton, "The Dramatist," 102.

14. Cordell, *Somerset Maugham,* 204.

15. Curtis, *Somerset Maugham,* 86.

16. Morgan, *Maugham,* 177, 186.

17. Calder, *W. Somerset Maugham,* 89.

18. Morgan, *Maugham,* 175.

19. Ibid., 177.

20. Ibid.

21. *New York Times,* 26 December 1913; in *Theatrical Companion to Maugham,* by Raymond Mander and Joe Mitchenson (New York, 1955), 111.

22. Ibid., 112–13.

Chapter Five

1. Anthony Curtis, *The Pattern of Maugham* (London, 1974), 27.
2. Ward, *Somerset Maugham,* 86.
3. Curtis, *Somerset Maugham,* 84.
4. Naik, *W. Somerset Maugham,* 45.
5. Maugham donated this manuscript to the Library of Congress in 1946 with the understanding that it would never be printed (he also at the same time donated the manuscript of *Of Human Bondage*).
6. *Of Human Bondage* (London, 1936); hereafter cited in the text as *OHB.*
7. Ward, *Somerset Maugham,* 58.
8. Calder, *W. Somerset Maugham,* 129, 91.
9. Ibid., 41.
10. Cordell, "Introduction," xi.
11. In *The Casuarina Tree* (London, 1926), 76–116.
12. Cordell, "Introduction," xviii.
13. Morgan, *Maugham,* 181.
14. Ibid., 181–82.

Chapter Six

1. Morgan, *Maugham,* 186.
2. William Somerset Maugham, *Don Fernando* (London, 1935), 198–99.
3. Calder, *W. Somerset Maugham,* 210.
4. Mander and Michenson, *Theatrical Companion,* 122.
5. Morgan, *Maugham,* 176, 192.
6. Ibid., 193.
7. Barbara Back, perhaps his closest female friend, would keep him informed of the ins and outs of London society in her numerous letters to him. ("Barbara Back was the exception to the rule that Maugham did not like women" [Morgan, *Maugham,* 294–95]).
8. "A Bitter Comedy on Our Expatriates," *New York Times,* 13 March 1917, 9.
9. Heywood Broun, "News of the Play World: Somerset Maugham Writes One Scene Far Off Key and Spoils 'Our Betters,' " *New York Tribune,* 13 March 1917, 11.
10. "After the Play," *New Republic,* 17 March 1917, 200.
11. "Our Betters," *New York Dramatic Mirror,* 24 March 1917, 7.
12. Channing Pollock, "Drama With a Domestic Finish," *Green Book Magazine,* June, 1917, 964–71.
13. " 'The Circle' at the Haymarket" *Graphic,* 12 March 1921, 320.
14. Louis V. De Foe, "Drama," *New York World,* 13 September 1921, 11.

15. Frank Swinnerton, "The Circle," *Nation and the Athenaeum,* 19 March 1921, 879–80.

16. Desmond MacCarthy, "Drama: 'The Circle,' " *New Statesman,* 19 March 1921, 704–5.

17. "Reviews: A Comedy of Manners," *Saturday Review* (London), 18 June 1921, 509.

18. *The Trembling of a Leaf* (London, 1921), 108; hereafter cited in the text as *TL.*

19. Brooks Atkinson, *New York Times,* November 30 1926, 26.

20. Raphael, *W. Somerset Maugham,* 62.

21. Curtis, *Somerset Maugham,* 122.

22. *Ashenden* (London, 1928), xvii; hereafter cited in the text as *A.*

23. *East and West* (London, 1934), xx.

24. Calder, *W. Somerset Maugham,* 220.

Chapter Seven

1. Cordell, *William Somerset Maugham,* 117.

2. Curtis, *The Pattern of Maugham,* 142.

3. The title, *Cakes and Ale,* is from Shakespeare's *Twelfth Night* (act 2, scene 3): Sir Toby Belch [to Malvolio]: "Dost thou think because thou art virtuous there shall be no more cakes and ale?" This title as well as the subtitle—"The Skeleton in the Cupboard"—concern Rosie. As Calder (*W. Somerset Maugham,* 193) observes, "Unlike Ted Driffield, Rosie is never extinguished by the forces of convention, and she remains the symbol of life as opposed to the sterility of the superficial literary society."

4. Paul Dottin, *William Somerset Maugham et ses romans* (Paris: Perrin, 1928).

5. Maugham to Paul Dottin, 1 January 1931, Humanities Research Center, University of Texas.

6. Ward, *William Somerset Maugham,* 157.

7. Seymour Krim, "Somerset Maugham," *Commonwealth,* 3 December 1954, 245–50.

8. Mark Van Doren, "Thomas Hardy Veiled," in *The Maugham Enigma,* ed. Jonas, 146.

9. Calder, *W. Somerset Maugham,* 334. 216; Calder states, "If 'Ashenden' and the 'I' of the short stories is a picture of the author as he would like to be, it reveals a great deal about Maugham, particularly about his attitude toward his relationships with his fellows."

10. Morgan, *Maugham,*

11. There is also a striking similarity between what Hardy does with *Tess of the D'Urbervilles,* and Maugham with Rosie. Both novels are unconventional views of the purity and virtuous nature of a woman who is what society considers a "fallen woman." Also, the involvement of the reader, although admittedly quite different in means, is strikingly similar in effect:

both involve the reader emotionally in the plight of an unusual heroine and cause the reader to wish, despite any misconduct on her part, that no harm will come to her.

12. In September 1931 Maugham sued Martin Secker, the publisher, for libel and Secker withdrew the book (Morgan, *Maugham,* 339–40). Depicted as Mr. Leverson Hurle, Maugham is portrayed as a writer who transfers friends, acquaintances, even strangers directly into his fiction, with little modifications of their personalities.

13. Calder, 179.

14. Katherine R. Fell, "The Unspoken Language of Edward Driffield," *Linguistics in Literature* 7 (1982):1–3.

Chapter Eight

1. Cordell, "Introduction," xi–xii.

2. Ibid., xii.

3. Some critics, such as Richard H. Costa ("Maugham's 'Partial Self': The 'Unexpected View' on the Way to 'The Death of Ivan Ilych,' " *CEA Critic,* May 1981, 3), find a "thou dost' protest too much" quality about what they call "Maugham's obsession" with the distinction between genius and talent ("genius": "Cervantes had an exceptional gift for writing; few people would deny him genius"; "talent": "Nor would it be easy . . . to find a poet with a happier gift than Herrick and yet no one would claim that he had more than a delightful talent" [*SU,* 75]). And Edmund Wilson complained that Maugham knows "something was going on, as on the higher ground . . . but he does not quite understand what it is, and . . . can never get up there." After contrasting Maugham's "Sanatorium" with Tolstoy's "The Death of Ivan Ilych," Costa praises Maugham for "the honesty and justice" of his "deepest imitations of himself and his craft." Wilson's statement about Maugham's inability to reach the higher road must be tempered by the fact that he spoke principally from ignorance, never having read Maugham's best works: *Of Human Bondage* or *Cakes and Ale* (see Morgan, *Maugham,* 501).

4. Calder, *W. Somerset Maugham,* 93.

5. *The Razor's Edge* (Garden City, N.Y.: Doubleday, 1944), 343.

6. Richard Ellman, *James Joyce* (New York: Oxford University Press, 1965), 1.

7. Graham Greene, "Book of the Day: Maugham's Pattern," *Spectator* 14 (January 1938).

8. Cordell, p. 1.

9. Maugham to editor, *Academy,* 11 September 1897.

10. Forrest D. Burt, "The Last of 'Willie' (To Richard A. Cordell, Willie's Friend)," a poem composed in 1969, dedicated to Richard A. Cordell, leading American Maugham critic since the 1930s.

Selected Bibliography

PRIMARY SOURCES

Ah King. London: Heinemann, 1936.
Altogether. London: Heinemann, 1934.
Ashenden. London: Heinemann, 1934.
Cakes and Ale. London: Heinemann, 1934.
The Casuarina Tree. London: Heinemann, 1935.
Catalina. London: Heinemann, 1935.
Christmas Holiday. London: Heinemann, 1941.
Collected Plays. Vol. 1. London: Heinemann, 1931. Contains *Lady Frederick, Mrs. Dot,* and *Jack Straw.*
Collected Plays. Vol. 2. London: Heinemann, 1931. Contains *Penelope, Smith,* and *The Land of Promise.*
Collected Plays. Vol. 3. London: Heinemann, 1932. Contains *Our Betters, The Unattainable,* and *Home and Beauty.*
Collected Plays. Vol. 4 London: Heinemann, 1932. Contains *The Circle, The Constant Wife,* and *The Breadwinner.*
Collected Plays. Vol. 5. London: Heinemann, 1934. Contains *Ceasar's Wife, East of Suez,* and *The Sacred Flame.*
Collected Plays. Vol. 6. London: Heinemann, 1934. Contains The Unknown, For Services Rendered, and *Sheppy.*
Cosmopolitan. London: Heinemann, 1938.
Creatures of Circumstances. London: Heinemann, 1950.
Don Fernando. London: Heinemann, 1937.
East and West. London: Heinemann, 1934.
First Person Singular. London: Heinemann, 1936.
The Gentleman in the Parlor. London: Heinemann, 1935.
Liza of Lambeth. London: Heinemann, 1932.
The Magician. London: Heinemann, 1956.
The Merry-Go-Round. London: Heinemann, 1949.
The Moon and Sixpence. London: Heinemann, 1935.
Mrs. Craddock. London: Heinemann, 1937.
The Narrow Corner. London: Heinemann, 1934.
Of Human Bondage. London: Heinemann, 1937.
On a Chinese Screen. London: Heinemann, 1935.
The Painted Veil. London: Heinemann, 1934.
The Razor's Edge. London: Heinemann, 1949.

The Summing Up. London: Heinemann, 1948.
Theatre. London: Heinemann, 1939.
Then and Now. London: Heinemann, 1959.
The Trembling of a Leaf. London: Heinemann, 1935.
Up at the Villa. London: Heinemann, 1967.
A Writer's Notebook. London: Heinemann, 1951.

SECONDARY SOURCES

1. Biography
Maugham, Robin. *Somerset and All the Maughams.* New York: New American Library, 1966. Background of family with emphasis on Somerset Maugham.
Morgan, Ted. *Maugham.* New York: Simon & Shuster, 1980. Most complete biography to date.

2. Bibliography
Sanders, Charles, ed. *W. Somerset Maugham: An Annotated Bibliography of Writings About Him.* Dekalb: Northern Illinois University, 1970. Helpful summary of criticism from 1897 to 1968, from non-English speaking countries as well.
Stott, Raymond Toole. *A Bibliography of the Works of W. Somerset Maugham.* London: Kaye & Ward, 1973. Definitive bibliography.

3. Book-length Studies
Barnes, Ronald E. *The Dramatic Comedy of William Somerset Maugham.* The Hague: Mouton, 1968. Study of the dramatic comedy with emphasis on structure and relation to society.
Calder, Robert. *W. Somerset Maugham and the Quest for Freedom.* London, Heinemann, 1972. Traces quest for freedom theme in the fiction; identifies Sue Jones as the basis for Rosie.
Cordell, Richard A. *Somerset Maugham: A Writer For All Seasons.* Bloomington: Indiana University Press, 1969. Contains material from 1937 and 1961 versions. A sound introduction to Maugham.
Curtis, Anthony. *The Pattern of Maugham.* London: Hamish Hamilton, 1974. General criticism of major works.
————. *Somerset Maugham.* London: Weidenfeld & Nicolson, 1977. Overview with illustrations.
Dobrinsky, Joseph. *La jeunesse de Somerset Maugham (1874–1903).* Paris: Didier, 1976. Treatment of early life and works; French influence, Freudian approach.
Jonas, Klaus, ed. *The Maugham Enigma.* New York: Citadel, 1954. Overview of literary accomplishments with critical essays.

————. ed. *The World of Somerset Maugham*. New York: British Book Centre, 1959. Critical essays.

McIvers, Claude. *William Somerset Maugham: A Study of Technique and Literary Sources*. Upper Darby, Penn.: The author, 1935. Traces the influence of Maupassant.

Mander, Raymond, and Joe Mitchenson. *Theatrical Companion to Maugham*. New York: Macmillan, 1955. Summary reviews, performance record, and illustrations of plays.

Naik, M. K. *W. Somerset Maugham*. Norman: University of Oklahoma Press, 1966. Traces conflict between "cynicism" and "humanitarianism" in the novels.

Raphael, Fredric. *W. Somerset Maugham*. New York: Charles Scribner's Sons, 1974. An overview of the life and works with illustrations.

Ward, Richard Heron. *William Somerset Maugham*. London: Geoffrey Bles, 1937. Uses Jungian principles; deals with Maugham's objectivity and subjectivity.

4. Articles

Archer, Stanley. "Artists and Paintings in Maugham's *Of Human Bondage*." *English Literature in Transition*, 1971. Explanation of Maugham's use of references to artists and their paintings.

Burt, Forrest D. "William Somerset Maugham: An Adlerian Interpretation." *Journal of Individual Psychology*, May 1970. Discussion of Maugham's life style and pattern of compensation.

Costa, Richard H. "A Pleasure Mr. Maugham." *Nimrod*, Fall–Winter 1976–77. Portrait of the elder Maugham.

————. "Maugham's 'Partial Self': The 'Unexpected View' on the Way to 'The Death of Ivan Ilych.' " *CEA Critic*, May 1981. Evaluative contrast of Maugham and Tolstoy.

Fell, Katherine Rowe. "The Unspoken Language of Edward Driffield." *Linguistics in Literature*, Fall 1982. Discussion of Maugham's use of nonverbal communication in *Cakes and Ale*.

Spence, Robert. "Maugham's 'Of Human Bondage': The Making of a Masterpiece." *Library Chronicle*, Spring–Summer 1951. Discussion of the history of the reception of this work.

Spencer, Theodore. "Somerset Maugham." *College English*, October 1940. Discussion of Maugham's strengths, especially his use of first person in fiction.

Index

Adler, Alfred, 12, 30, 32–36
Ah King (Maugham), 23
Alanson, Bertram, 21, 24, 25, 103
Aldington, Richard, 23
Allen, Walter, 51
Arnold, Matthew, 11, 38
"The Artistic Temperament of Stephen Carey" (Maugham), 16, 25, 28, 71, 73, 74–75
Ashenden (Maugham), 22, 111–14, 116, 126

Back, Barbara (Ivor), 138
"A Bad Example" (Maugham), 16
Barrymore, Ethel, 109
Bennett, Arnold, 6
Books and You (Maugham), 24
Brontë, Emily, 130
Brooks, John Ellingham, 11–12, 94
Browning, Robert, 97
Burt, Forrest D., 10
Butler, Samuel, 41

Cakes and Ale (Maugham), 6, 7, 17, 19, 21, 22, 24, 25, 79, 94, 107, 114, 115–33, 137, 138, 139, 140
Calder, Robert, 36, 48, 49, 55, 57, 65, 78, 97, 114, 115, 122, 123
Carlyle, Thomas, 38, 53
Casuarina Tree, The (Maugham), 22
Catalina (Maugham), 24, 25
Chaucer, Geoffrey, 51
Christmas Holiday (Maugham), 23
Churchill, Winston, 26
Circle, The (Maugham), 21, 22, 24, 103–105, 118
Congreve, William, 101–102
Connolly, Cyril, 10, 19
Constant Wife, The (Maugham), 21, 22, 109–111, 118
Cordell, Richard A., 23, 24, 39, 63, 79, 85, 115, 135, 136, 141

Cosmopolitan (Maugham), 23
Coward, Noel, 13, 17–18
Creatures of Circumstances (Maugham), 24
Crowley, Aleister, 19
Curtis, Anthony, 6, 9, 10, 50, 65, 71, 72, 110, 115

"Daisy" (Maugham), 16
Dante, Aligheri, 11
Day, Martin, 25
Dickens, Charles, 25, 78
Dobrinsky, Joseph, 56
"A Domiciliary Visit" (Maugham), 111–12
Don Fernando (Maugham), 23, 96, 134
Dottin, Paul, 29, 118, 134
Doubleday, Nelson (Maugham), 24
Dryden, John, 37, 115

East and West (Maugham), 111, 112
Ellmann, Richard, 139
The Explorer (Maugham) 19, 63

"The Fall of Edward Barnard" (Maugham), 106
Fell, Katherine R., 125
Fielding, Henry, 11, 78
Fisher, Kuno, 11, 82
Fitzgerald, Edward, 11
Flaubert, Gustave, 42
Fleming, Ian, 26
Forster, E. M., 13, 24

Galsworthy, John, 23
Gauguin, Paul, 97–100
The Gentleman in the Parlour (Maugham), 21
Gissing, George, 41
Goethe, Johann, 41
Goldsmith, Oliver, 100
Great Novelists and Their Novels (Maugham), 24, 25

Greco, El, 96
Greene, Graham, 140

Hardy, Thomas, 44, 45, 97, 123
Hawtrey, Charles Henry, 37–38
Haxton, Gerald, 12, 21, 25, 28, 59,
    94, 95, 100, 102, 103, 105, 110,
    123
The Hero (Maugham), 18
Highet, Gilbert, 38
"The Human Element" (Maugham), 57

Ibsen, Henrik, 11
Isherwood, Christopher, 13

Jack Straw (Maugham), 19, 63
Jones, Ethelwyn Sylvia ("Sue"), 19, 20,
    22, 25, 59, 65–66, 72, 85, 91, 94,
    95, 102, 105, 123
Jones, Henry Arthur, 16, 19
Jonas, Klaus, 26
Joyce, James, 71, 139

Kant, Immanuel, 15
Kelly, Grace, 26
Kelly, Sir Gerald, 85
Kipling Rudyard, 37
Kubrick, Stanley, 68

Lady Frederick (Maugham), 19, 20, 28,
    58–63, 70
The Land of Promise (Maugham), 20,
    65, 66–70, 72, 94, 114
The Land of the Blessed Virgin
    (Maugham), 18, 99
The Landed Gentry (Maugham), 63
Lang, Andrew, 52
Lawrence, D. H., 55, 71
The Letter (Maugham), 22
Liza of Lambeth (Maugham), 16, 28,
    30, 41, 42–51, 58, 118, 140
Loaves and Fishes (Maugham), 59, 63
"Looking Back" (Maugham), 6, 7, 10,
    11, 27, 28, 95

McDonnell, Angus, 20
McIver, Claude, 154
Macaulay, Thomas, 38
MacCarthy, Desmond, 105

Machiavelli, Niccolo, 52
The Magician (Maugham), 19
The Making of a Saint (Maugham), 18,
    52–54, 58, 97, 118, 126
A Man of Honour (Maugham), 19, 59
Mander, Raymond, 154
Marriages Are Made in Heaven or Schiff-
    bruechig, 57
Maugham, Edith Mary Snell, 1–3
Maugham, Frederic, 1–4, 28
Maugham, Henry Macdonald, 4, 6
Maugham, Liza, 21, 28, 94, 100
Maugham, Robert Ormond, 1–3
Maugham, Robin, 25, 28
Maugham, Syrie (Wellcome), 20–21,
    27, 28, 59, 65, 66, 72, 91, 93, 94,
    95, 100, 101, 102, 103, 110–111,
    123
Maugham, W. Somerset: beginning of
    a career, 40–51; birth and childhood,
    1; birth of his daughter, Liza, 21;
    burden of life and composition of Of
    Human Bondage, 20–21, 64–66;
    comic novel, 116–22; compensation
    and sources, 122–23; completion and
    assessment of work, 22–27; develop-
    ing the dramatized narrator, 97–101,
    126–133; divorce from Syrie, 21;
    dramatic skill in fiction, 74–79; early
    education, 8–10; education in Hei-
    delberg, 11; experimentation in writ-
    ing, 51–55; fame and anxiety, 1940–
    65, 23–27; homosexuality, 11–13;
    loss of faith, 13; love affair with Sue
    Jones, 20; marriage to Syrie Well-
    come, 21; medical training, 15–16;
    orphaned and loss of nurse, 4; period
    of greatest productivity and changes:
    1915–1930, 21–22; persona, 30–31,
    78, 122; reading, 8, 11; reshaping
    life, 71–74; style of life, 28, 30–37;
    stammer, 5–6; theatrical success,
    59–64; use of dialogue, 79–82,
    123–25; use of nonverbal communi-
    cation, 125–26; writing an accom-
    plished novel: Of Human Bondage,
    55–58
Maupassant, Henri, 10, 142
May, Rollo, 15

Meredith, George, 11
Mill, John Stuart, 71
"Miss King" (Maugham), 112–14
The Mixture as Before (Maugham), 24
The Moon and Sixpence (Maugham), 21, 95, 97–101, 103, 105, 106, 114, 115, 118, 126, 135, 137, 139
Morgan, Ted, 5, 8, 11, 12, 25, 57, 65, 67, 91
Morris, William, 47
Morrison, Arthur, 41
Mrs. Craddock (Maugham), 18, 54–56, 58, 68, 79, 118
Mrs. Dot, 19

The Narrow Corner (Maugham), 23
Newman, John Henry Cardinal, 11, 71

Of Human Bondage (Maugham), 5, 6, 7, 20, 21, 22–23, 24, 25, 26, 28, 30–35, 41, 45, 49, 50, 55, 64, 66–67, 71, 72–93, 94, 96, 97, 99, 100, 101, 102, 111, 115, 118, 122, 123, 124, 132
On a Chinese Screen (Maugham), 21
Orientations (Maugham), 18, 21, 106
Our Betters (Maugham), 21, 79, 101–103, 105, 118
"The Outstation" (Maugham), 79, 114

The Painted Veil (Maugham), 21, 59
Pater, Walter, 11, 38
Pfeiffer, Karl, 14, 26
Phelps, William Lyon (Maugham), 25
Pinero, Arthur, 58
Points of View (Maugham), 26
"The Punctiliousness of Don Sebastion" (Maugham), 18, 30
Purely for My Pleasure (Maugham), 27

Queen Elizabeth, 26

"R" (Maugham), 111
"Rain" (Maugham), 103, 107–109, 114
Raphael, Frederic, 2, 3, 4, 48, 55, 57, 109
The Razor's Edge (Maugham), 17, 24, 36–37, 57, 95, 97, 106, 114, 134, 137–139

Riposte, A. or Mordaunt, Elinor (pseudonym for Evelyn May Wiehe), 123
Rossetti, Dante G., 47

St. Augustine, 71
Schiffbruechig. See Marriages Are Made in Heaven
Schiller, Johann, 36
Scott, Sir Walter, 78
Searle, Alan, 12, 26, 28
Selfridge, Gordan, 65, 91, 101
Shakespeare, William, 65, 75
Shaw, George Bernard, 23
Sheppey (Maugham), 23, 134
Sheridan, Richard, 100
Stern, G. B., 138
Stevenson, Adlai, 26
Swift, Jonathan, 37
Swinburne, Algernon, 11
Swinnerton, Frank, 23
The Summing Up (Maugham), 6, 23, 24, 28, 37, 53, 58, 95, 134–136

The Tenth Man (Maugham), 63
Theatre (Maugham), 23, 57
The Trembling of a Leaf (Maugham), 21, 103, 106–109

Unwin, Fisher, 52
Up at the Villa (Maugham), 24

The Vagrant Mood (Maugham), 26
Vaihinger, Hans, 36
Van Doren, 118
Verlaine, Paul, 11
Voltaire, François, 37

Wagner, Richard, 11
Ward, Richard Heron, 14, 23, 41, 48, 71, 72, 78, 118
Wellcome, Syrie. *See* Maugham, Syrie Wellcome
Wells, H. G., 23
Westcott, Glenway, 12, 40
Wilde, Oscar, 13, 17, 58
Wilson, Edmund, 26
Writer's Notebook (Maugham), 25, 63, 64, 46
The Writer's Point of View, 51